Contours of Christian Philosophy
C. STEPHEN EVANS, *Series Editor*

Contours of Christian Philosophy
C. STEPHEN EVANS, *Series Editor*

Metaphysics

Constructing
a World View
William Hasker

InterVarsity Press
Downers Grove, Illinois, U.S.A.
Leicester, England

InterVarsity Press
Box F, Downers Grove, Illinois 60515, U.S.A.
38 De Montfort Street, Leicester LE1 7GP, England
© *1983 by Inter-Varsity Christian Fellowship of the United States of America*

InterVarsity Press, U.S.A., is the book-publishing division of Inter-Varsity Christian Fellowship, a student movement active on campus at hundreds of universities, colleges and schools of nursing. For information about local and regional activities, write IVCF, 233 Langdon St., Madison, WI 53703.

Inter-Varsity Press, England, is the publishing division of the Universities and Colleges Christian Fellowship (formerly the Inter-Varsity Fellowship), a student movement linking Christian Unions in universities and colleges throughout the British Isles, and a member movement of the International Fellowship of Evangelical Students. For information about local and national activities in Great Britain write to UCCF, 38 De Montfort Street, Leicester LE1 7GP.

The poetry on p. 30 is from "The Road Not Taken" from The Poetry of Robert Frost *edited by Edward Connery Lathem. Copyright 1916,* © *1969 by Holt, Rinehart and Winston. Copyright 1944 by Robert Frost. Reprinted by permission of Holt, Rinehart and Winston, Publishers, New York, and by Jonathan Cape Limited, London.*

ISBNs: USA 0-87784-341-4   USA 0-87784-339-2 (Contours of Christian Philosophy set)
*   UK 0-85110-715-X*

Printed in the United States of America

Library of Congress Cataloging in Publication Data

Hasker, William, 1935-
  Metaphysics, constructing a world view.

  (Contours of Christian philosophy)
  Includes bibliographical references.
  1. Metaphysics.   I. Title.   II. Series.
BD111.H276   1983   110   83-10693
ISBN 0-87784-341-4

British Library Cataloguing in Publication Data

Hasker, William
    Metaphysics.—(Contours of Christian philosophy)
    1. Metaphysics
    I. Title   II. Series
    110   BD111

    ISBN 0-85110-715-X

20   19   18   17   16   15   14   13   12   11   10   9   8   7
99

to Arthur Holmes,
my first teacher of philosophy

GENERAL PREFACE

The Contours of Christian Philosophy series will consist of short introductory-level textbooks in the various fields of philosophy. These books will introduce readers to major problems and alternative ways of dealing with those problems. These books, however, will differ from most in that they will evaluate alternative viewpoints not only with regard to their general strength, but also with regard to their value in the construction of a Christian world and life view. Thus, the books will explore the implications of the various views for Christian theology as well as the implications that Christian convictions might have for the philosophical issues discussed. It is crucial that Christians attain a greater degree of philosophical awareness in order to improve the quality of general scholarship and evangelical theology. My hope is that this series will contribute to that end.

Although the books are intended as examples of Christian scholarship, it is hoped that they will be of value to others as well; these issues should concern all thoughtful persons. The assumption which underlies this hope is that complete neutrality in philosophy is neither possible nor desirable. Philosophical work always reflects a person's deepest commitments. Such commitments, however, do not preclude a genuine striving for critical honesty.

C. Stephen Evans
Series Editor

AUTHOR'S PREFACE

Any brief book on metaphysics must be selective, and I have preferred to treat a limited number of issues with some adequacy rather than skim superficially over a larger number. All of the topics treated belong to what Michael Scriven has called "primary philosophy"—they are problems "to which everyone has an answer, whether he knows it or not, and which everyone can understand, whether he has tried to or not." The book's primary purpose is to serve as one of several texts in an introductory philosophy course. It might also be used as a core text in a course on metaphysics, though such a course would have to include some topics which are omitted here. Finally, I hope the book may be of use to the interested reader outside any formal course framework. That is to say, I hope there are not too many passages which are so obscure as to absolutely require the assistance of an instructor to explain them!

My obligation to other writers will, I am afraid, be all too obvious; probably not even all of my mistakes are original! Among my teachers I should like to single out Arthur Holmes, to whom the book is dedicated. For many years he has been for me a model of a Christian philosopher, scholar and educational statesman. Much of whatever merit the book may possess is due to my students, who over a number of years have helped me to understand which issues are most important to them, and how these issues can be most understandably presented. C. Stephen Evans, the series editor, has been immensely helpful with advice, criticism and encouragement throughout the project. My son Robert read an early draft and helped me to see what needed to be said more clearly. Keith Yandell also gave helpful comments on the entire manuscript, and his criticisms triggered some important improvements.

Finally, an immense debt of love and gratitude is owed to my wife, Nancy, my sons, Robert and Kevin, and my dog, Gunpowder, all of whom had to put up with me while I was writing this book.

I

Introducing Metaphysics

*W*hat is there?" According to an eminent philosopher these simple words suffice to formulate the central question of all metaphysics.[1] And his answer is even simpler: "Everything." Obviously this is correct; whatever there is, is included in "everything," while whatever doesn't exist is really "nothing." But it's also obvious that both question and answer need much more explanation. So, let's break the question "What is there?" down into some more specific questions—questions to which metaphysics will try to give detailed answers.

Metaphysical Questions

First of all, *what is real?* We all distinguish between things that are real, that really exist, and things that aren't real. We can apply this distinction to persons, such as Paul Bunyan and Wyatt Earp; to activities, such as beaming aboard the Starship Enterprise and flying at supersonic speeds from Paris to New York: or to places, such as the land of Narnia and the Grand Duchy of Monaco. The second member of each pair, we say, is real or really exists, while the first member isn't and doesn't. Other examples are controversial: Is the Loch Ness monster real or not? And what of the yeti, the abominable snowman of the Himalayas? Some people believe in the reality of one or both of these, while others deny it and still others reserve judgment.

These, however, are still not the sorts of cases to which philosophers apply themselves when they ask what is real. But consider these questions: Is there such a being as God? Is a human being endowed with an immaterial self or "soul" which survives bodily death? Is there such a thing as a person's performing an act of free choice, an act which is not determined or controlled by anything at all except the person's own decision? Such questions as these take us right to the heart of metaphysics, and we will be concerned with all of them later in this book.

Second, *what is ultimately real?* What are the *basic constituents* of reality? We are familiar with the idea that things can be broken down into their constituents—for instance, a lovely perfume can be analyzed as a mixture of various organic chemicals, and these in turn as combinations of atoms of the various chemical elements, and so on. We tend to feel as we work through such an analysis that we are gaining insight into the real nature of what we are studying, that we are finding out what is "really real" in it. And we could almost define metaphysics by saying that a metaphysician is someone who pushes this kind of question just as far as it can go—to find the "ultimate reals" out of which are constructed perfumes and skyscrapers and planets and social structures and indeed simply everything.

Often this analysis of real things into their constituents is carried on in scientific terms, but a metaphysician may want to ask whether the constituents identified by science are the "ultimate reals," or whether they can themselves be analyzed in terms of something still more basic. Sometimes what seems to be a strange or even preposterous statement about what is real turns out, when properly understood, to be instead a claim about what is "ultimately real." Thus when a philosopher says that physical objects don't exist, he probably doesn't mean to say that there are no such things as trees, tables and baseball bats. It's much more likely that what he means is that the "ultimate constituents" of such objects, what they really consist of, is something very different from physical objects as we ordinarily think of them. Perhaps trees and ball bats are ultimately made up of mental images, thoughts in people's minds. Of course, this may still strike you as being strange and implausible, but it isn't so obviously false and absurd as it would be to deny outright the existence of physical objects.

One may also ask whether the constituents identified by science are *all* of the "ultimate reals" that go to make up something. For instance, a physiologist can give an analysis of visual perception in terms of the focusing of reflected light by the lens of the eye, the reaction to this light by the rods and cones of the retina, the transmission of the visual information through the optic nerve and the processing of this information within the brain. But does this analysis include *all* of what is involved in seeing something? That is an important—and highly controversial—question of metaphysics.

Throughout these last paragraphs I have been assuming that we can indeed discover what is ultimately real by breaking things down into their constituents. But according to one group of philosophers this approach is fundamentally mistaken. The theory of *wholism* claims that wholes, complex entities, typically have a reality of their own over and above that of their constituents. Thus, analysis of a whole into its parts always falsifies its nature by failing to capture this "something more." According to extreme forms of wholism, the *only* ultimately correct answer to the question "What is there?" would be "everything." Any other answer would distort the truth by failing to capture the indissoluble unity of the Real (or, as some would say, of the Absolute). In this book I shall assume that the process of analysis is valid and that we can find out what a thing is by determining what it consists of. But the reader should be aware of the existence of the wholistic viewpoint.

Finally, metaphysics asks, *what is man's place in what is real?* Out of all the different sorts of beings in heaven and earth, there is no doubt that we have a very special interest in the creatures we ourselves are, namely, human beings. That concern partly, no doubt, expresses our self-centeredness, and it is tempting to wonder what philosophy would be like if it were written by an ant or an electron. On the other hand, it just is a fact that in the world as we know it human beings are somewhat unique. Ants and electrons, after all, *don't* write philosophy, and this is part and parcel of the reasons why both are several notches below humans in what has been called the "great chain of being." If, on the other hand, we someday find that there really are extraterrestrial intelligences, their philosophical views will be of the deepest interest.

For the part of the universe we know, however, humans would seem to be either the highest, most complex and elaborate products of nature, or else the visible link between nature and something beyond nature: "mid-way between the brutes and the angels," as Pascal put it. Which of these is true (or, conceivably, whether both might be true) is clearly a question of great importance. It will have significance for what we sometimes call the meaning of life, for how we ought to live and for what (if anything) we ought to worship. Not all the questions in this area, to be sure, are questions of metaphysics; some belong to ethics, some to the philosophy of religion and some to still other disciplines. But metaphysical questions—questions about what there is—lie at the very core of these issues. They are among the enduring questions of philosophy because they are among the central —and ultimately inescapable—issues of human life.

All these types of questions are illustrated in this book. Chapter two, "Freedom and Necessity," asks about the real existence of causally undetermined acts of human free choice. Chapter three, "Minds and Bodies," poses from several different directions the question of the ultimate constituents of human beings, their experiences and their actions; it also asks about the real existence of the immaterial, immortal human soul. Both of these chapters in their different ways contribute to our understanding of man's place in what is real.

In chapter four, "The World," we wrestle with the question of the ultimate constituents of the natural world and the implications of this for our understanding of science and the universe as a whole. Chapter five, "God and the World," deals with that Being whose real existence is both supremely important and intensely controversial. It also takes up the relationships between that Being and the created world; thus it sets the stage for a final consideration of man's place in what is real.

These are not all of the questions of metaphysics but they are, I believe, the most important ones. They are questions which are vital for each one of us as we go about the task of constructing a world view. We need to think as clearly and accurately about them as we possibly can.

Answering Metaphysical Questions
If the topics suggested here are some of the central questions of metaphysics, how shall we go about answering them? Unfortunately, this question can't be answered in a way all philosophers would accept. Philosophers disagree about the correct methods for resolving philosophical questions almost as much as they disagree about the answers to the questions. So it's not possible to give a complete account of the "right" philosophical method without taking sides between the various philosophers and philosophies—something I hardly want to do so early in this book! For present purposes I shall compromise by giving an account of philosophical method which is general enough to be acceptable (as far as it goes) to most philosophers, and yet specific enough to

be of some help as we deal with various metaphysical questions in the subsequent chapters.

To begin with something absolutely fundamental, in philosophy we are seeking to have *good reasons* for the assertions we make. All of us have some beliefs that we accept on the basis of prejudice, or hunches, or because someone once told us it was so, or even just out of habit. When we are philosophizing, however, we won't base our statements on such beliefs as these; instead, we will try to stick to what we have *good reason to believe*. Does this mean that all our statements must be proved? No, it doesn't. To see why not, we must consider briefly the meaning of "proof." Speaking generally, we prove that something is true if we can show its truth by reasoning *based on other things we know to be true*. That is to say, a proof is a special kind of *argument*, a process of reasoning whereby, on the basis of a statement or statements already known or assumed to be true (the premises), we are able to justify some new statement (the conclusion).

Now whatever we can prove (or have a strong argument for), we have good reason to believe; but not everything can be proved. In order to prove anything, we need to have premises which we already know (or have good reason to believe) to be true. Some of these premises may be things we have established by previous arguments, but not all of them can be. For in that case in order to prove anything, we should first have to prove the premises of our proof—but to do *that* we must first have proved the premises for *that* proof—and so on indefinitely. Obviously this is impossible, so if there is anything we have good reason to believe, there must be some things which we are entitled to take as true without first having proved them.

But what are these basic or foundational truths, as they are sometimes called? This is one of the central questions of the branch of philosophy known as *epistemology*, or the theory of knowledge; we certainly can't try to settle it here.[2] For our present purposes we can best operate on the basis of a couple of rules of thumb which will enable us to proceed without first settling the question of which truths are basic.

The first rule is this: *We may take as premises for a metaphysical argument anything we know, or have good reason to believe, to be true.* This would certainly include ordinary perceptual beliefs, such as my belief that I am now seeing a tree, as well as the many sorts of beliefs that are justified through sense perception, including beliefs about historical facts and the well-established results of science (always to be carefully distinguished from the speculations, conjectures and opinions of scientists). Another broad category of beliefs can be classified under the headings of logic ("No statement can be both true and false") and mathematics ("7 + 5 = 12"; "If equals are added to equals, the results are equal"). These seem to be justified not by sense perception, but by some sort of rational insight or understanding.

There are still other beliefs which don't readily fit into any of these categories. For example: "Nothing begins to exist without a cause." This is something all of us seem to believe, but what are our grounds for accepting it? We might be tempted to think it is justified through experience, but actually this is very questionable. Just what experiences have we had that entitle us to assert concerning every single thing in the universe, that if this thing has not always existed then something caused it to exist? Things do sometimes make their appearance inexplicably, and if we decide to look for the cause we are not always successful. Our conviction that there must be a cause somewhere, even if we can't find it, seems to be a conviction we *bring to* our experience, rather than a conclusion *drawn from* experience. On the other hand, there doesn't seem to be anything logically contradictory in the idea that an object should just originate spontaneously out of nothing. So why are we so convinced that this can't happen?

That nothing begins to exist without a cause is just one example of the sort of belief I am referring to. Another example is this: "Nothing we do now can change the past." This also is not something we can very plausibly claim to have learned through experience, nor does it seem possible to prove it without assuming as a premise some other principle which is less obvious than the thing we are trying to prove. The status of principles such as these has been and continues to be a hotly debated issue in metaphysics and epistemology. And once again, it's an issue that I can't attempt to settle in an introductory chapter. For our present purposes, the best way of looking at such principles will be to consider them as *metaphysical data,* that is, as fundamental assumptions that we seem to bring to experience rather than derive from it, and which we seem firmly to believe in without being able to prove.[3] Such beliefs are not immune to challenge, if anyone wants to challenge them (in philosophy, *nothing* is immune to challenge!). But certainly they must be taken very seriously in any attempt we make to reason out the nature of the world in which we live.

We have now identified, in a rough and general way, several kinds of beliefs that we are entitled to assume as premises in metaphysical arguments. But is there any guarantee that by following these guidelines we shall arrive at *truth* and at conclusions which are acceptable to all reasonable people? The answer is that there is no absolute guarantee of this. Notoriously, one person's unchallengeable truth is another's questionable assumption, and for someone else it may be an outright falsehood. This is not to say that "truth is relative," but simply to point out that there is no person or group of persons whose belief in a statement can be taken as an absolute guarantee that the statement is true.

This leads to our second rule of thumb for doing metaphysics: *No belief, no matter how firmly held or apparently well supported, is beyond the possibility of challenge or questioning.* Another way of putting this is to say that philosophy is, ideally, a completely nondogmatic subject. Nothing is accepted merely on authority, no matter how reputable; and no assertion, however outrageous, is ruled out of court if it can be supported with good reasons.

The point about the role of authority or authorities in philosophy requires more discussion. One might be tempted to say that authority has no place at all in philosophy, but this can't be entirely true. None of us lives life or forms beliefs without considerable reliance on authorities of various kinds. It is important to distinguish the various kinds of authorities and see how they function.

One type might be termed *legal authority;* in this I include not just the law in a narrow sense but rather all situations in which some person or group of persons has the right simply to *decide* something which henceforth is so just because it has been decided that way. Thus a network executive has authority to decide whether a soap opera will be pre-empted in order to cover a presidential news conference, the city council has authority to determine what shall be the speed limit in residential areas, and so on. Now legal authority, in spite of its great importance for life in general, has no place at all in metaphysics, nor, for that matter, in science or mathematics. These disciplines deal with matters which are as they are independent of any decisions which can be made by human beings (a point which seems to have escaped the notice of the state legislature which, as legend has it, passed a law fixing the value of the mathematical constant π!).

But this is not the only kind of authority. Such fields as science, history and medicine, while not based on legal authority are nevertheless heavily dependent on authorities of another kind. Obviously a historian could do nothing if he were not prepared to rely on the authority of those who have witnessed past events. It is perhaps less obvious that scientists rely on authority, but it is true all the same: A scientist would be hopelessly handicapped if, before she could make use of an established scientific law or theory, she had first to repeat for herself the experiments by which its truth was established. Nor could a physician proceed without relying on case studies, experimental data and other information which inform him of the benefits (and possible dangers) of the course of treatment he is undertaking.

There are differences in the nature and roles of the authorities in these cases, but they can all be placed under the heading of *expert authority:* They are cases in which certain persons are relied on for information because of special experiences or expertise. Now it would be most unreasonable for us to deprive ourselves of expert authority when doing metaphysics, for in doing so we would also deprive ourselves of a great deal of knowledge that is otherwise available to us, and some of this knowledge might prove to be crucial in answering metaphysical questions. There are, however, three important points to notice concerning this reliance on expert authority: (1) The authorities involved are ordinary human beings exercising ordinary human capacities and methods of gaining knowledge, although perhaps developed to an extraordinary degree. (2) The knowledge derived from the authority is knowledge which could (in principle if not always in practice) be checked and confirmed (or disproved) by some other person. (3) The claims made by the authority can in the end still be rejected if we have weighty enough reasons for doing so. Expert authority really is authoritative, but it is not absolute. And reliance on it does not introduce into metaphysics any objectionable dogmatism or authoritarianism.

One other kind of authority needs to be considered: I refer to *religious authority,* in which truths are proclaimed by God or by someone authorized to speak on behalf of God. Clearly this is quite different from both kinds of authority considered so far. It differs from legal authority in that it not only renders decisions which determine how matters shall stand (though it may do this), but also gives information concerning situations which are as they are prior to, and independent of, the authoritative pronouncement. God's creating the heavens and earth out of nothing did not take place as a result of his having declared the creation to Moses! And it differs from expert authority in that the knowledge conveyed is not solely the result of ordinary human abilities exercised by ordinary human beings, nor is it regarded as being subject to disproof by further research.

Now it should be clear on the basis of what has been said that religious authority cannot be accepted as a basis for philosophical assertions. To do so would mean that a great many of the questions of metaphysics, including some of the most important ones, would be questions no longer; they would be settled dogmatically by the religious authority. Philosophy would no longer be a free and independent investigation of fundamental issues; it could at most be an exercise in working out the implications of unchallengeable truths derived from an external source. And of course the problem would arise that people are by no means agreed concerning the religious authorities they accept or the way they interpret them; in practice, the result would be that philosophy could no longer be carried on as a common human endeavor, but would instead become a fragmented enterprise carried on by the various faith communities largely in isolation from each other. In short, it would no longer be philosophy.

But while it is clear that philosophical assertions can't be based on religious authority, it is less clear what our reaction to this situation ought to be. Some religious persons conclude that philosophy must be entirely rejected, that it is purely and simply a result of man's sinful rebellion against his Maker. Alternatively, they may insist that philosophy should be carried on along the lines sketched in the previous paragraph: It should begin by accepting the truths of divine revelation and proceed to develop a comprehensive world view on that basis. On the other hand, many secular philosophers interpret the situation as an indication that religion (and specifically Christianity) is nonrational and perhaps even antirational—that one simply must choose between being a believer and settling things by a nonrational faith, and being a philosopher and thinking things out rationally.

All of these reactions, I believe, are mistaken. To begin with, there *is* a discipline in which believers begin by accepting the truths of revelation and proceed to interpret these and to develop them into a systematic view of things. But the name of this discipline is theology, not philosophy. The demand that philosophy should proceed along these lines is simply the demand that philosophy be replaced by theology. But what of the idea, common to both the believer and the unbeliever as depicted above, that there is a fundamental incompatibility between philosophical inquiry and faith?

In order to see why this is wrong, we need to make some distinctions. The first is the distinction between the *content* of one's belief and the *reasons* for that belief—between *what* is believed and *why* it is believed. The religious beliefs held by a Christian philosopher will be essentially the same as those held by any other orthodox Christian believer. But in his philosophical work he is concerned not with the validation of these truths through divine revelation, but with what can be said about them (as well as about other things) on the basis of ordinary human methods of understanding and inquiry. This suggests a second distinction—a distinction between one's final, overall conclusions about the way things are, and what can be ascertained through the methodology of a particular discipline. To take an obvious example, a physicist (it is to be hoped) will have some views about the proper way to conduct himself in his relationships with his family and friends, but he will not expect to establish these views as the result of his study of physics. And the Christian philosopher will hold to a belief in the Incarnation of God in Jesus Christ, but he need not expect to establish this truth as the conclusion of a philosophical argument.

But what, you may ask, is the *need* of philosophy for the Christian? In a sense, this entire book is an answer—or part of an answer—to this question. For now, let me say just two more things. First, beginning early on, Christian theology has made extensive use of philosophy, including pagan philosophy, in developing and interpreting the Christian revelation; the influence of philosophy on theology has become so pervasive that even theologians who consciously reject philosophy (for example, Karl Barth) cannot escape it. Second, there is a widespread conviction among Christians—expressed in the often-heard phrase "the integration of faith and learning"—that there is a need to think through the relationships of all branches of knowledge to the Christian faith, so as to produce an integrated Christian view of things that will be functional in the modern world. But it is impossible that such an integrated view will come about without making heavy use of the resources of philosophy. If philosophy did not already exist for this purpose, it would have to be invented.

Let me conclude this section on a more personal note. The author of this book is a Christian who loves philosophy and would like to consider himself a philosopher; he is a philosopher who loves Jesus Christ and wants to be known as a disciple. A Christian first, a philosopher second—but neither one at the expense of the other. The insights I have gained from my Christian faith and experience prove to be of immense value as I do my philosophy, even though I cannot appeal to biblical authority as the basis for a philosophical argument. And the results of philosophical study enhance Christian understanding in many different ways—some of them already hinted at, others yet to be shown.

Evaluating Metaphysical Theories

The last section focused, however briefly, on some of the "nuts and bolts" issues concerning how philosophical views are built up, attacked and defended. But it is also helpful to step back and take a broader view. This we can do by asking how metaphysical theories are to be evaluated. By a metaphysical theory I mean simply a well-thought-out answer to a metaphysical question. Such a theory could consist of a single sentence, or it could be developed in an elaborate treatise. Such theories, I suggest, function for us in ways that are similar, though not identical, to the functioning of scientific theories; they serve to unify areas of our experience and make them understandable to us. If this is so, then it ought to be possible to evaluate metaphysical theories using criteria which are similar to those used for scientific theories, and this is indeed the case: Metaphysical theories can be judged on the basis of their *factual adequacy, logical consistency* and *explanatory power*. We will consider these one by one.

Metaphysical theories must be *factually adequate*. Like scientific theories they must be in agreement with the facts about the subject matter with which they are concerned. Unfortunately, what counts as a "fact" in metaphysics is itself a matter of controversy. This is essentially the same problem discussed in the previous section when we asked what sort of statements can be taken as premises for metaphysical arguments. But it is clear that a metaphysical theory, to be acceptable, must be consistent with what you know by other means to be true, and a theory which is inconsistent with what everybody knows (if there *is* anything which is known to everyone!) cannot be acceptable to anyone.

I said before that metaphysical theories function in ways that are similar, but not identical, to the functioning of scientific theories. This is a good place to point out the difference between them. Scientific theories must be *predictive* and *testable;* that is to say, it must be possible to use the theory to predict the results of observations which have not yet been made, and then the theory is tested by seeing whether the actual results agree with the predicted results. In general this cannot be done with metaphysical theories; indeed this may be the most important difference between the two kinds of theories. (According to philosopher of science Karl Popper, science is "falsifiable metaphysics"!) Note, however, that this difference draws the line between science and metaphysics at a given time, not necessarily for all time. The hypothesis that physical objects consist of atoms had very little predictive power when it was first introduced by some ancient Greek philosophers, but it is now an integral and highly predictive part of modern physical science.

A second requirement is that metaphysical theories, like scientific theories, must be *logically consistent*. Of two statements which are logically inconsistent with each other, at most one can be true; and a theory which contains or implies two such statements has something seriously wrong with it. Unfortunately, inconsistent theories usually don't wear their inconsistency on their sleeve; often the inconsistency is subtle or hidden, and it can be a matter of some difficulty to determine whether an inconsistency is actually present. Note also that proving a theory inconsistent doesn't necessarily mean that everything asserted by the theory is wrong. Sometimes an inconsistent theory can be restored to consistency by modifying it in minor ways, while leaving the rest of the theory pretty much unaffected. But the criterion of logical consistency is an important one in evaluating theories of all kinds.

The third criterion for metaphysical theories is *explanatory power*. This requirement is sometimes combined or confused with factual adequacy, but the two are clearly distinct. Suppose, for example, a physicist has been conducting a series of experiments on radioactive decay and has compiled an exhaustive set of records giving the conditions and results of each experiment. When we ask him to explain his results, he simply hands over his records of the experiments. Clearly, he hasn't done what we asked of him, but why not? His records, we may assume, contain no logical inconsistencies, and they fit the facts as well as anyone could desire —better, in fact, than any theory that could be provided. (Agreement between theory and observations is always approximate, never absolute.) But however admirable in both these respects, the scientist's records are totally lacking in explanatory power. They do nothing, that is, to unify the experimental data with each other or with other knowledge in the field; they give us no hint of the causes of the observed phenomena; they give us no sense whatever that we have comprehended what is going on. The feeling of insight, of enlightenment, that is the subjective accompaniment of understanding, is entirely lacking.

It must be admitted that this criterion of explanatory power is somewhat less precise and clear-cut than the requirements of factual adequacy and logical consistency. At least part of the reason for this is that explanatory power as I have described it is a combination of several attributes that, ideally, all come together in a good theory but which also may trade off against each other in some cases. Among these attributes I have mentioned that a good theory should serve to *unify* the data to be explained and that it should if possible identify the *cause* which accounts for them. Other characteristics which contribute to explanatory power are the breadth, or *comprehensiveness,* of a theory and its *simplicity.* A theory which succeeds in bringing together within a single framework realms of experience that were previously unrelated represents a distinct gain in explanatory power. (One of Newton's greatest achievements was that he brought together under a single explanatory scheme the previously separate fields of terrestrial and celestial mechanics.) Simplicity is also a valuable attribute of any theory. A theory in which the explanation is as complicated, or almost as complicated, as the facts to be explained represents little if any gain in explanatory power.

So the notion of explanatory power is complex and difficult to characterize precisely. Yet there can be no doubt that explanatory power is real and that it plays an important part in the evaluation of both scientific theories and metaphysical theories. A satisfactory theory, in the final analysis, must be one which satisfies our desire to *understand.*

2

Freedom
and
Necessity

*W*e deeply desire to be free, but what is freedom? Is it a matter of being allowed to do whatever we choose? Does freedom mean primarily being able to choose our own government or our own personal lifestyle? Or is freedom mainly a matter of being safe from certain ominous and threatening evils—freedom from disease, from poverty, from oppression?

Freedom is of all these things and more, for "freedom" is a word with many meanings. There is political freedom, which is expressed and affirmed in such documents as the Magna Charta and the Declaration of Independence. There is economic freedom, currently the focus of so many social and political conflicts. There is emotional freedom, that happy state in which we are in touch with our own feelings and able to express them easily and naturally. There is the spiritual freedom of which the apostle Paul wrote so eloquently in the letter to the Romans.

Are We Really Free?

None of these kinds of freedom, however, is the focus of the present chapter; it is concerned rather with *freedom of choice,* or *freedom of the will.* Probably all of us have felt, as we have confronted some important decision, that it is entirely up to us how things will go. Soon the decision will be made and we will live with its consequences, but for now the future lies soft and malleable in our hands. And sometimes later, as we look back at such moments, they seem to be charged with immense importance. As Robert Frost said, "Two roads diverged in a wood, and I—/I took the one less traveled by,/And that has made all the difference."[1] We sense, as we look back at such turning points, that in those moments we determined our own destiny.

But is this really so? In making those significant choices, and innumerable lesser ones, were we, in fact, creating a future which remained indeterminate until we had made our choice? Or were we rather carrying out or enacting a scenario which had long before become inevitable, perhaps from the beginning of time? A great many reasons have been given why the experience of free choice cannot really be what it seems to be. Isn't it absurd to say that when we make choices, there is *no reason whatever* why we choose one way rather than another? But if there is such a reason, then doesn't this negate the idea that in making choices we, as it were, create our future out of nothing? And isn't this talk of creating out of nothing something which verges on blasphemy? Only God has this power, and it is necessary to think of ourselves and all the events and decisions of our lives as lying entirely within his control. Omar Khayyám was a Muslim, but he spoke for a great many Christians when he wrote:

With earth's first clay they did the last man knead,
And there of the last harvest sowed the seed:
And the first morning of creation wrote
What the last dawn of reckoning shall read.[2]

In addition to religious objections to freedom of choice, there are scientific considerations which suggest that our decisions are by no means as free as they seem. From psychology we learn about reinforcement and conditioning, and about childhood experiences which have made us what we are. From biology we learn of genetic determinants of behavior and of biochemical balances in the brain which determine everything from fleeting moods and emotions to our very sanity. From physics we learn to see ourselves, our society, our entire planet, as a tiny part of an inconceivably vast universe which is ruled throughout by immutable physical laws. Nowhere in this picture is there room for a person, an individual human being, who determines what shall take place in his own life without regard to the necessary relationships of cause and effect in the universe as a whole.

This, then, is the problem of freedom and necessity; it is a problem which arises because of the conflict between our sense of freedom and the many reasons which seem to suggest that our actions are not free but rather necessitated—by God, by fate, and by natural causes of various kinds. The problem is deeply fascinating considered merely as an intellectual question, but surely it is much more than this. Many people will tend to think of freedom of choice as something valuable, something which gives to their lives a significance which they would otherwise not possess. Others will see the belief in free will as an expression of pride and of absurd self-importance and will find deep satisfaction in the view that each thing we do and that happens to us is part of the immutable order of the universe.

It is very plausible to suppose that our belief that persons are responsible for their actions—that they deserve praise and reward when they do well, and blame and punishment when they do badly—can only be correct if it is also true that they are free in acting as they do, so that the action is not necessitated by anything other than the person's own choice. But it may be replied that this belief in responsibility is itself a dangerous illusion, an illusion which at best tends to impede intelligent thought about the treatment of persons who manifest socially deviant behavior, and which at worst becomes a cloak for savage and irrational vengeance against those who have injured us. We hardly need to be reminded of how strong the feelings run on both sides of this issue.

So far we have been content to characterize the conflicting views in somewhat vague and imprecise ways, but in order to proceed we must from now on become more accurate. Let us define *determinism* as the view that *for every event which happens, there are previous events and circumstances which are its sufficient conditions or causes, so that, given those previous events and circumstances, it is impossible that the event should not occur*. Notice that the definition does not say anything specific about the *nature* of the previous events and circumstances which necessitate the given event. This is deliberately left open because there are several different varieties of determinism which take different views on this point. But they all agree in holding that everything which happens is necessitated.

In contrast with determinism, the view of those who affirm free will is *libertarianism,* defined as the view that *some human actions are chosen and performed by the agent without there being any sufficient condition or cause of the action prior to the action itself.* Notice that the definition claims that free actions have no *sufficient* cause, not that they lack causes and conditions altogether. If you offer to sell me your old car, and I decide to accept, then your making the offer is certainly a *condition* of my accepting it, and it may qualify as a partial *cause* of my acceptance. But it is not a *sufficient* cause, because it does not *necessitate* my acceptance. Even after you had offered, with all the other circumstances exactly as they were, it was still entirely within my power either to accept your offer or to reject it. Notice also that the definition does not claim that *all* human actions are free in this sense, but only that *some* are. It is quite possible for the libertarian to admit that in some cases (for instance, those in which there is overwhelmingly strong motivation pushing a person in one direction only) no action is possible other than the one which was actually taken. The determinist, on the other hand, claims that *all* actions are determined.

As we proceed we will add further qualifications and explanations of these two positions, as well as others. But these definitions are adequate for now.

Compatibilism: A Way Out?

In the discussion so far we have been assuming that there is a logical incompatibility between free will and determinism, so that accepting either one means giving up the other. Quite a number of philosophers, however, have questioned this assumption. The position of *compatibilism,* or *soft determinism,*[3] holds that *there is no logical inconsistency between free will and determinism, and that it is possible that human beings are free and responsible for their actions even though these actions are causally determined.* This compatibilist view is "soft" determinism because it enables one to accept determinism without accepting the radical conclusions (denial of free will and moral responsibility) drawn by other ("hard") determinists.

Now it is obvious that this position, if it is viable, offers great attractions. For many of us, at least, the belief that we are free and responsible persons seems extremely important; it is a belief we could give up only under extreme pressure, and even then only with a sense of great loss. On the other hand, we have also seen that there are weighty considerations favoring determinism, so we seem to be faced with a serious intellectual conflict. If, however, the apparent inconsistency between freedom and determinism is *only* apparent, the situation changes immediately. The preparations for all-out conflict can be replaced with an agreement for peaceful coexistence or détente.

But can the peace treaty be signed? It is clear that free will *as defined by the libertarian* cannot be reconciled with determinism, for one view affirms the existence of events which lack sufficient causal antecedents, while the other denies this possibility. So one would expect that, in order to maintain his thesis of compatibility, the soft determinist must be defining "freedom" in some other way.

This is indeed the case. According to compatibilism, a human action is free if it exhibits the following characteristics: (1) It is not caused by compulsion or by states of affairs external to the agent. (2) Instead, the *immediate cause* of the action is a psychological state of affairs internal to the agent—a wish, desire, intention or something of the sort. (3) The situation is one in which it was *in the agent's power* to have acted differently, *if he had wanted to.* (Some compatibilists prefer to say "if he had willed to" or "chosen to." But these variations make no essential difference to the argument.)

An action fitting this description may well be called free. The agent had alternatives and was not forced to take one rather than the other; he did what, in that situation, he most wanted to do, and if he had wanted to do something else he would have done that instead. And for such an action one may well be held responsible, and punished if one has chosen wrongly—for the cause of the action lies in the character and personality of the agent, and this may be correctable through punishment. (If, on the other hand, the cause were external to the agent, it could not be corrected by punishment, which would then be pointless.) And of course none of this implies that a free and responsible action lacks a sufficient cause.

Unfortunately, this solution is illusory. To see this with regard to responsibility, consider an example: Max, a seventeen-year-old high-school dropout, has been caught stealing a set of hubcaps from an auto supply store. All the conditions given above for a free and responsible action are satisfied. Nothing forced Max to take those hubcaps; he took them because he wanted them, because his old hubcaps were scratched and rusty. Now according to determinism there is, immediately prior to Max's taking the hubcaps, a set of events and circumstances which together constitute a *sufficient condition* of his taking them—such that, given those events and circumstances, it is impossible that he should not steal the hubcaps. We will call this set of events and circumstances the *proximate cause* of Max's stealing the hubcaps. Max's desire to have new hubcaps, and his belief that he could not get them any other way, will be an important part of the proximate cause; this is what, according to the compatibilist, makes the action a free and responsible one.

Now this desire and belief, as well as the other elements in the proximate cause, are themselves the result of previous causes; these will include events in Max's life—things he has said and done, and which other people have said and done to him, as well as other things which have affected him. But since *every* event, according to determinism, has prior sufficient causes, we can go on tracing the chain of causes backward until we have arrived at a set of events and circumstances which together constitute a sufficient condition for the occurrence of the proximate cause, and *all of which occurred before Max was conceived and born.* Call this set of events and circumstances the *prior cause.* The prior cause is, as we have said, a sufficient condition for the occurrence of the proximate cause, and since the latter is a sufficient condition for Max's act of stealing the hubcaps, it follows that the prior cause is also a sufficient condition for Max's theft.

Now let us ask a few questions about Max's responsibility. Is Max responsible for the occurrence of the prior cause? How could he be, when all of the events and circumstances in the prior cause occurred when he did not yet exist? Is Max responsible for the fact that *if the prior cause occurs, Max's theft of the hubcaps must also occur?* Again, clearly not. That this is so is a result of those immutable laws of nature which, according to determinism, govern everything which takes place and which Max had no part in establishing and no power to overrule. Finally, is Max responsible for stealing the hubcaps? How could he be responsible? The act of stealing is causally necessitated by the events and circumstances of the prior cause, to which Max contributed nothing at all. And given that the prior cause did occur, Max could no more prevent its inevitable outcome—his stealing the hubcaps—than he could stay the planets in their courses or stop the crustal plates of the earth in their relentless march across the ocean floor. So determinism and moral responsibility just *are* incompatible, and that is that.

But what about freedom? The criteria of free action set forth by the compatibilist are certainly significant, but are they sufficient to guarantee free agency in the sense which is important to us? In supporting an affirmative answer to this, the compatibilist emphasizes that in his view the agent, when acting freely, does what he wants to do, and that *if he had wanted* to choose differently, he could have done so. But how, we ask, could he have wanted something other than what he did want? Perhaps the answer is that he could have, if he had acted differently on some earlier occasion. If Max had gotten a paper route when he was twelve, instead of hanging around the electronic-game arcade, he would have formed the habit of working for things and would have wanted to earn the hubcaps instead of stealing them.

But could he have acted differently *then*? The answer, once again, is that he could have if he had wanted to! And now we see where the soft determinist is leading us—nowhere. When asked whether someone could have chosen differently, the answer is that he could have, *if* something else had been different. But the truth is that the something else which would have had to be different *could not* have been different than it was, for it was itself the result of prior conditions in accordance with inescapable natural law. The compatibilist is able to make his analysis of free choice seem adequate only so long as he keeps our attention focused on the immediate situation, in which Max stole the hubcaps because he wanted to and could, if he wished, have refrained from stealing them. But as soon as we place this situation in its larger causal context, we see that Max's desires and inclinations, his personality and character, are themselves the inevitable result, according to ineluctable laws of nature, of causal antecedents which existed before he was even born. And the illusion of freedom vanishes.

Determinism: Arguments and Objections

So free will is incompatible with determinism; we are forced to choose—freely or not!—between them. In this section some of the main arguments for the determinist position will be considered, as well as objections to those arguments. In the next section, libertarianism will receive the same treatment. In these two sections we will concentrate on philosophical arguments for the two sides, leaving theological considerations for the concluding section of the chapter.

Before going into the arguments for determinism, it is necessary to remove some misconceptions about the determinist position. To begin with, it must be emphasized most strongly that *determinists do not deny that people make choices.* If they did deny this, their position would be absurd, but the fact is they do not. Furthermore, the *experience* of choosing—of seeing alternatives, weighing their desirability and finally making up one's mind—is not any different whether one is a libertarian or a determinist. For while determinists believe that there *are* sufficient conditions which will govern their choices, they do not know at the time when they are making a decision *what* those determinants are or *how* they will decide as a result of them. So, like everyone else, they simply have to make up their own minds! The difference between libertarian and determinist lies in the *interpretation* of the experience of choice, not in the experience itself.

Another misconception of the determinist position is that, according to determinism, "our choices don't make any difference." This suggests an image of a determinist as one who drives wildly on dangerous mountain roads, because "whatever will be, will be." Now it may be that there are a few determinists who think and behave like this, but this approach to life is certainly not implied by determinism. A determinist, to be sure, believes in a sense that whatever happens is inevitable. But it does *not* follow from this, that whatever happens is inevitable, *regardless of what I do*. For this to be true my own choices and actions would have to be entirely disconnected from the rest of what goes on, so that they make no difference to anything else that happens. But this, far from being implied by determinism, is actually inconsistent with it. So a determinist, if he understands his own position, will be as concerned as anyone to avoid known dangers and to work hard for desired outcomes—only, unlike the libertarian, he regards his own efforts, choices and actions as inevitable parts of the necessary and unalterable order of things. Once again, the difference is not so much in the experience itself as it is in the interpretation of the experience.

But what are the arguments for determinism? For some (perhaps many) determinists, determinism seems to have the status of an ultimate principle. It is, in the sense described in chapter one, a metaphysical datum. Leibniz, for example, found the "principle of sufficient reason" to be a necessary truth of reason; this principle states that for anything which occurs, there must be some sufficient reason why *that* thing occurs rather than something else. And really, how can this be doubted? If there is no *sufficient* reason for something to happen, then this means that the reasons that actually exist are *insufficient*—and if that were so, the event would not take place.

When this is applied specifically to human choices, the result is what is sometimes called *psychological determinism*—the doctrine that our choices are governed by whatever, in the given situation, is our strongest motive. Suppose you have a decision to make—say, between taking a week's vacation or getting in another week of work before school starts again in the fall. Obviously, there are motives pulling you in both directions. You need the vacation, but you also need the money you could earn. For a while the two motives may seem to be equally balanced. But eventually one of the two turns out to be stronger, and that is what determines your decision. If this didn't happen, how could you ever decide? From the medieval logician Jean Buridan we have the sad tale of "Buridan's Ass," who starved to death between two equidistant piles of hay because he had no "strongest motive"—no "sufficient reason"—to determine him to choose one rather than the other.

Arguments such as these have considerable weight, but for many determinists the strongest reasons for their position come from the theory and practice of modern science. The most general scientific argument for determinism is found in the claim that determinism is a "methodological assumption," a "necessary presupposition" of science. The scientist is seeking to understand, explain and control nature. The way to reach this goal is by discovering and stating the universal laws to which natural processes conform. The scientist, to begin with, does not know what the laws are; that is what he or she is trying to determine through investigation. But it is absolutely essential to assume *that* such laws exist—that is, that determinism holds—for if he or she does not assume this, the whole endeavor makes no sense at all. And of course all this applies as much to the science of human behavior as to any other part of science. Thus, B. F. Skinner states, "You can't have a science about a subject matter which hops capriciously about. Perhaps we can never *prove* that man isn't free; it's an assumption. But the increasing success of a science of behavior makes it more and more plausible."[4]

This general scientific argument for determinism is buttressed by arguments derived from the results of the specific sciences. From physics we derive the picture of the universe as a huge physical mechanism—the "clockwork universe," as it used to be called. While our understanding of the details of the mechanism has changed over the years, the overall picture retains a strong appeal. According to the nineteenth-century physicist and mathematician Laplace, a sufficiently powerful intelligence

> knowing, at a given instant of time, all forces acting in nature, as well as the momentary positions of all things of which the universe consists, would be able to comprehend the motions of the largest bodies in the world and those of the smallest atoms in one single formula. . . . To it, nothing would be uncertain, both future and past would be present before its eyes.[5]

And of course men and women—their blood and bones, their muscles and nerves—are very much a part of this universal mechanism, subject to the same physical laws as a grain of sand or a galaxy.

Other sciences add confirmatory results. Biology, including genetics and biochemistry, offers an increasingly detailed, though still far from complete, account of how the universal mechanism of nature works itself out in the lives and behavior of human beings. Freudian psychoanalysis points out that a good deal of human behavior is controlled by unconscious motivation, which is unknown to the agent and certainly not under voluntary control. Psychological behaviorism, already represented in the quotation from Skinner, explains human and animal behavior as the result of classical or "Pavlovian" conditioning and "operant conditioning." Sociology adds to this its own insights concerning how our beliefs, desires and behaviors are molded by the social context of our lives. And so on.

Not all of these scientific results are equally well established (the scientific status of Freudian psychology, for example, is far less secure than that of biochemistry), but each adds its contribution to a cumulative picture of a universe which is lawful throughout. Is it not absurdly pretentious, in light of all this, for humans to consider themselves and their plans and decisions an exception to this universal causal order?

So the case for determinism—seemingly a powerful one. But things are not always what they seem! When examined more closely, the arguments for determinism turn out to be open to serious objections, which greatly lessen their force and in some cases destroy it altogether.

To begin with, the argument that determinism is a "necessary presupposition of science" seems clearly unsound. Note first of all that the presupposition is relevant to the work of the scientist only if he is committed to finding and formulating laws which are strictly *deterministic*—that is, laws which assert that in a given set of conditions exactly *one* result can and must follow. But many fields of science seem to get along quite happily with *statistical* laws which assert merely that, out of a number of cases of a certain kind, a *certain percentage* will yield a specific result. Of course, it might be said that this simply reflects the immature and unsatisfactory condition of those sciences, that the statistical laws are merely temporary stand-ins for the deterministic laws that represent our ultimate goal.

But even if we were to concede that the final aim of the scientist must be the formulation of deterministic laws, this by no means justifies our assuming the truth of determinism! What it does justify is the claim that *if success is possible in a certain field of science* (where "success" is defined as the discovery of true, deterministic laws), *then there must be deterministic laws which hold true of the phenomena of that field.* But whether success is possible can only be found out by looking; only the faint-hearted will need to have success guaranteed in advance by a "metaphysical postulate" of determinism! As Bertrand Russell said, "A physicist looks for causes; that does not necessarily imply that there are causes everywhere. A man may look for gold without assuming that there is gold everywhere; if he finds gold, well and good, if he doesn't he's had bad luck. The same is true when the physicists look for causes."[6]

So the argument for determinism as a methodological assumption of science is unconvincing. Nor is the support from the specific sciences as impressive as it might seem. Physics in particular, having been for centuries the chief support of the determinist, has now become a major embarrassment. The picture of the clock-work universe, though gradually modified (for example, by the discovery of electromagnetic radiation), is a fair summary of the physicist's view of the world from about 1650 until 1925. But the discovery by Heisenberg in that year of the "uncertainty relations" changed things fundamentally by introducing theories according to which the behavior of the ultimate physical particles is governed by chance and is predictable only in probabilistic terms. Even after this "physics of chance" was well established scientifically, a good many philosophers and scientists clung to the hope that this situation represented merely a temporary state of physical theory and that indeterministic theories would be replaced by those postulating determinism at a still deeper level. Well known is Einstein's dictum that "God doesn't play dice." But Einstein seems to have been wrong about this; a recent series of experiments seems to have demonstrated that there can be no "hidden variables" and that indeterminacy is fundamental.[7]

It is important to be clear about the implications of this. The proof of physical indeterminacy does not by itself establish the reality of free will; the causally undetermined appearance of a photon at one point rather than another can hardly be viewed as an instance of free choice! And it is possible, though by no means certain, that physical indeterminacy never has any perceptible effect on the actions of human beings. But even on the most favorable reading, determinism has suffered considerably. These developments would seem to have exploded once and for all the notion that the only proper goal of science is to search for deterministic laws: The progress of physics, clearly the most advanced science, has led it in the opposite direction. And insofar as determinism has for hundreds of years found its strongest support in the physical world-picture, the advocate of a deterministic view of human action is forced to ask himself just what good reasons he still has for the position he is advocating.

Such support will hardly be found in the sciences of human behavior, for no such science has come anywhere close to establishing deterministic laws of behavior which would permit accurate prediction in individual cases. At best the sciences of behavior have established valid statistical generalizations, and sometimes (for example, in psychoanalysis) even this is lacking. Now some scientists, such as Skinner, and even some philosophers point to these statistical generalizations as evidence that underlying deterministic laws exist and await our discovery. But this is entirely fallacious. The existence of statistical regularities *in no way* constitutes evidence for an underlying determinism. Modern physics with its indeterminism, and indeed the mathematical theory of probability itself, demonstrate conclusively that it is possible to make highly reliable statistical predictions (for example, gambling odds) based on the assumption that the behavior of individual units (dice, playing cards) is governed entirely by chance. Now of course the existence of statistical laws is *consistent* with an underlying determinism, just as it is consistent with the assumption that chance is fundamental. But the statistical laws of behavioral science, while they are *consistent* with a deterministic view of human action, can by no means provide *evidence* for such a view.

Nor is support for determinism to be found in the psychological determinist's claim that "we always act on the strongest motive." This claim, which at first seems substantive and significant, turns out on analysis to be empty and devoid of meaning. To see this, consider the determinist's reaction to an apparent counterexample, a situation in which a person has acted contrary to what we would have assumed to be her strongest motivation—and perhaps has done this for no reason that we can discern. Does the determinist say, "Oh, well, maybe in this case we have an exception; apparently she did *not* act on her strongest motive"? By no means; what he says is, "We *thought* that her strongest motive was so-and-so, but now we see that it was not." And he will say this *even if the actual motive is completely unknown!* This shows clearly that the determinist identifies the strongest motive as "the motive which, in fact, leads to action." Thus his claim reduces to the triviality that we always act on the motive which we act upon!

We are left, finally, with the claim that determinism is an ultimate rational truth, that the occurrence of undetermined events is in the end simply inconceivable. Insofar as this claim is simply asserted without argument, it is difficult to refute by argument. But if determinism is viewed as a position to be supported by evidence, it must be said that the evidence is far from conclusive.

Free Will: Arguments and Objections

For libertarianism, as for determinism, it is necessary to begin by removing some misconceptions. First, it is not true, as is sometimes alleged, that a libertarian conceives of a free choice as a chance event. A free choice is a *choice:* that is, it is an event in which alternatives are noted, considered, evaluated in terms of some kind of criteria, and finally decided one way or the other. The libertarian differs from the determinist in that the determinist affirms that there must be *sufficient causes* which determine the agent to choose as he does, while the libertarian denies this. But this denial in no way places a free choice in the same category as a random event.

To amplify this a bit, a libertarian in no way denies the relevance of motive to human choices, nor does she deny that it is possible to influence actions by presenting the agents with relevant motivations (rewards, punishments and the like). So the argument, common since the time of Hume, that only determinism can account for the efficacy of rewards and punishments, is wide of the mark. Libertarianism does not, indeed, accept the statement that "we always act on the strongest motive." The problem with this (as noted in the previous section) is not so much that it is false as that it is vacuous, in that we do not, in general, have any independent way of measuring which motive is strongest, other than by observing how the agent actually behaves. In many cases it is more illuminating to say, not that our action is determined by the strongest motive, but rather that *we* determine the strength of our motives by determining which motives to attend to. Thus when we are weighing a question of conscience it often makes good sense to say that *it is we who decide* whether personal convenience or moral obligation shall weigh more heavily with us.

But supposing that free will is a coherent thesis, what reason is there for supposing it to be true? One reason, certainly a weighty one for many libertarians, lies in *the very experience of choice,* as described earlier in this chapter. This experience seems to carry with it the strong conviction that the various alternatives are indeed within our power—that there is nothing at all which prevents us from choosing one way or the other. Some philosophers, indeed, have found in this the complete and sufficient demonstration of freedom of choice. Thus Descartes said: "[It] would be absurd to doubt that of which we inwardly experience and perceive as existing within ourselves."[8]

In saying this, however, Descartes goes too far. The experience of choice may be vivid and dramatic and may very well engender in Descartes the conviction that his will is free in the full libertarian sense. But there is no way that Descartes can guarantee, by introspective awareness alone, that sufficient causal conditions for his action are lacking. The experience of choice is not, by itself, a proof of the existence of free will.

On the other hand, I would maintain that the intuitive conviction of freedom, sustained as it is by the occurrence of choices in which we seem to determine our own future, is one that we are entitled to take seriously and to treat with great respect as we formulate our answer to the question of freedom and necessity. This is particularly true in that, as we have seen, the arguments for the deterministic view are far from compelling. Our conviction of freedom could, for all that, turn out to be an illusion. But why suppose that it is?

A second argument in favor of free will can be stated as follows: *If all human actions are causally determined, then no one is ever morally responsible for any action.* But in many cases people *are* morally responsible for their actions. Therefore, not all human actions are causally determined. The argument for the first premise has already been given above and need not be repeated here. The determinist, therefore, must simply deny that people are ever responsible. Sometimes this denial is buttressed by the observation that emotive considerations such as our desire to believe in moral responsibility should have no bearing on such a topic as determinism.

This seems to me to be misguided in several respects. First, it is not a question simply of *wanting* to believe in moral responsibility; all of us, libertarians and determinists alike, have experienced occasions on which we would have preferred *not* to be held responsible. (And note that I do not reciprocate by charging the determinist with a desire to escape from responsibility.) But many of us share a deeply held conviction that it is true that we are responsible for our actions, *whether we like it or not.* Of course, if it were perfectly clear on other grounds that freedom of choice is an illusion, perhaps we would have to bite the bullet and give up our belief in responsibility. But as we have seen, things are just not that way. And why is this deeply held conviction about responsibility less entitled to respect, less eligible to be considered as a metaphysical datum, than the determinist's belief that determinism is true? Which belief is really harder to give up? It would appear that a great many people manage to live very comfortably without a belief in determinism. The belief in responsibility, on the other hand, is so deeply wrought into the fabric of society that it is extremely difficult even to imagine, let alone to implement, a social order that would dispense with it entirely. If a determinist does not seek to visualize *and to implement* such a changed order of society, he would seem to be open to the charge that his commitment to determinism is less than fully serious.

However that may be, it seems that the issue of moral responsibility in relation to free will is one of those deep-lying differences which mark the turning points in metaphysical thinking. Rational argument, however lucid, is unlikely to settle such issues to the satisfaction of all concerned. The motives for the opposing views are too deeply rooted and too tenaciously held. All the metaphysician can do, in such a case, is to clarify as thoroughly as possible the opposing views, the logical relations between them and the arguments for each—and then make his choice.

This section will conclude with yet another argument against determinism and in favor of free will, one which is of a somewhat different sort than those considered so far. For one thing the argument may be a bit more subtle and difficult than the others; it is also unique in that it is directed at a specific kind of determinism rather than at determinism in general. But the conclusion of this argument is a powerful one, so that if the argument is sound the determinist is in deep trouble.

The argument begins with a reflection on the nature of rational thinking, the kind of thinking one is engaged in when (as now) one seeks to evaluate evidence and arrive at a conclusion justified by the evidence. It is clear, when we consider the matter, that rational thinking must be *guided by rational insight* in the light of principles of sound reasoning. That is to say, one must "see," rationally, that the conclusion is justified by the evidence—and one is helped to see this by principles of reasoning, such as the laws of inductive and deductive logic and the like. Furthermore, and this point is crucial, one accepts the conclusion *because* one recognizes that it is justified by the evidence. It is this recognition which brings about the acceptance.

Now let us suppose that all human thinking is physically determined in the following sense: (1) Every thought or belief accepted by a person is a result of that person's brain being in a corresponding state. (2) We assume, provisionally, that the physical indeterminacy which exists at the quantum level makes no perceptible difference in the overall functioning of the brain. So that the brain functions, in effect, as a deterministic system. It follows that (3) every brain state, and therefore every thought and belief of the person, is fully determined by the physical functioning of the brain in accordance with the deterministic laws of physics.

Is it not evident, on this supposition, that rational thinking is an impossibility? It cannot be true, on this assumption, that anyone's thinking is guided by rational insight; rather, it is guided entirely by the physical laws which govern the brain's functioning, which proceed with no regard to whether the thought processes they generate correspond to principles of sound reasoning. Occasionally, to be sure, it may happen that the thought processes generated by the physically determined functioning of the brain will arrive at a conclusion which is correct. But this, when it happens, is simply a fortunate accident—and to say that a conclusion is reached by accident is incompatible with the claim that that conclusion was reached by rational thinking. Therefore, if all human thought is physically determined, then no one ever thinks rationally.

Nor is the situation changed if we modify our assumptions (and our definition of "physically determined") so as to allow that sometimes random, physically undetermined events within the brain have a perceptible effect, so that a different conclusion is reached than would have been the case without the random event. For such a random event is no more responsive to rational insight than was the physically determined brain process of the previous model. What is needed for rationality is not simply an injection of *randomness* into the physically deterministic brain functioning, but rather an infusion of *rational insight* as a factor which guides and directs the thought processes. But to accept this is to give up physical determinism altogether. And so our conclusion: *If physical determinism is true, no one ever thinks rationally.*

This conclusion is naturally difficult for the determinist to accept! It means that if he continues to affirm his determinism, he must admit that our belief that we are capable of rational thinking is an illusion—and this, of course, includes the determinist's own thinking, the thinking by which he justifies his determinism as well as everything else he believes! The alternative, of course (surely the more *rational* alternative?), is to abandon determinism.

So far as I have been able to find out, no determinist has yet produced a satisfactory answer to this argument. Perhaps the most common move is to claim that the argument confuses *reasons* for belief with *causes* of belief, and to point out that a conclusion may be *supported by* reasons (and therefore rational) without those reasons having *caused* the acceptance of the belief. But if my recognition that there are good reasons for a belief is not what *brings about* my acceptance of the belief, then I am not rational in accepting it. And this is so even if there *are* good reasons for it which might lead someone else to accept it rationally. But if physical determinism is true, no one ever accepts a belief because she sees that it is supported by good reasons.

Another response to the argument is to point to the existence of computers to establish that a physically determined process can be rational. Computer processes undoubtedly are physically determined, yet it is in no way a "fortunate accident" that they reach accurate results. This is true, but not really damaging to the argument. Computers function as they do *because they have been constructed by human beings endowed with rational insight*. And the results of their computations are accepted *because they are evaluated by rational human beings as conforming to rational norms*. A computer, in other words, is merely an extension of the rationality of its designers and users; it is no more an independent source of rational thought than a television set is an independent source of news and entertainment.

It seems clear that the last word has not been spoken on this argument. In fact it has only recently begun to get the attention it deserves. At present, however, it stands as a critical (and, in my opinion, still unresolved) difficulty for physical determinism.[9]

Freedom, Necessity and God

We turn finally to the question which was deliberately passed over until now: What has God to do with the issue of free will and determinism? It would hardly be feasible to omit this question altogether; religious considerations play an important role for many people in determining their views of free will. Yet the question seems to create something of a dilemma for philosophy, a dilemma related to the separation of philosophy from theology, as indicated in chapter one. It is hardly possible to consider the question without presupposing various theological doctrines concerning God and his decrees. But how is it possible to do this without introducing religious authority and thus erasing the boundary between philosophy and theology?

Actually, however, this dilemma is not too difficult to resolve. We shall indeed deal with the free will issue in the light of various theological doctrines, but we shall present these doctrines not dogmatically or assertively, but rather hypothetically. We shall not say, "God decrees that so-and-so, and therefore such-and-such follows," but rather, "*If* we assume that God decrees so-and-so, then such-and-such follows from that." In this way we are able to see what follows philosophically from various theological doctrines while recognizing that the doctrines themselves are accepted, if at all, on other than philosophical grounds. Of course, it is possible that as we proceed in this manner some of my own theological preferences will become apparent! But this, if it happens, will just have to be put up with. In any case it should be clearly recognized that each of the alternative views discussed in this section has been affirmed and defended by some Christians and rejected by others. The issue of freedom and necessity is one on which a Christian consensus does not exist.

First of all, let us consider the doctrine of *predestination,* the doctrine that God, in his sovereign wisdom, effectively determines everything which takes place. God is not thought of as decreeing that certain things shall happen in response to the free and autonomously decided actions of his creatures, for this would place the ultimate power of decision in the creatures, with God reduced to the role of responding to an already given situation. As Augustine said, "The will of God is the necessity of things."

It is quite clear that the doctrine of predestination entails determinism: specifically, *theological determinism*. God has effectively determined everything that shall happen, and no creature has the power to act otherwise than God has decreed. It is clear, furthermore, that the theological determinist, at least if he is a Christian, must be a soft determinist, for the view that humans are responsible for their actions is central to Christian belief. Thus one has the very difficult problem, discussed above, of explaining how a person is responsible for his actions when he was unable to act otherwise. And there is the additional problem of explaining how God himself is *not* responsible for human wrongdoing, even though it is God's decrees which necessitate that the wrongdoing occurs. Whether there are satisfactory solutions to these problems probably depends on further theological considerations which cannot be pursued here; we only mention the problems in passing.

Suppose, though, that one does not affirm universal divine predestination. Unfortunately, the Christian who wishes to be a libertarian is not yet out of the woods! People will often say that God does not *determine* our actions, but he nevertheless *knows* in advance exactly what we will do. But there is a strong argument which seems to show that divine *foreknowledge* is just as inconsistent with free will as is predestination. Suppose, for instance, that I am going to have a cheese omelet for breakfast tomorrow. We can then construct the following argument:

1. It is now true that I will have a cheese omelet for breakfast tomorrow. (Assumption)

2. It is impossible that God should at any time believe anything false or fail to believe anything which is true.[10] (Assumption: divine omniscience)

3. Therefore God has always believed that I will have a cheese omelet for breakfast tomorrow. (Inference from 1 and 2)

4. If God has always believed a certain thing, it is not in my power to bring it about that God has not always believed that thing. (Assumption: the inalterability of the past)

5. Therefore it is not in my power to bring it about that God has not always believed that I will have a cheese omelet for breakfast tomorrow. (Inference from 3 and 4)

6. It is not possible for it to be true both that God has always believed that I will have a cheese omelet for breakfast tomorrow, and that I do not in fact have one. (Inference from 2)

7. Therefore it is not in my power to refrain from having a cheese omelet for breakfast tomorrow. (Inference from 5 and 6)

So I do not have free will with respect to the decision whether or not to eat an omelet.

The argument can also be summarized briefly as follows: I cannot now change what God has always believed about what I will do, nor is it possible for me to act in a way that would contradict God's belief about me. So I have no free will—in this case, or in any other.[11]

Can this argument be refuted? It is often pointed out that one cannot reasonably assume that God's knowing (or believing) what I will do causes me to act accordingly. But the argument makes no such assumption. The argument does indeed imply that God's belief is a *sufficient condition* of my acting accordingly; this is just to say that it is impossible for God to believe in one way and for me to act in another. What, if anything, *causes* my action is left as a problem for further investigation.

There are various other attempts to evade the force of this argument, but we cannot go into them now. The fact is, as it seems to me, that the argument as it stands is entirely valid, so that the only legitimate way to escape from the conclusion is to deny one of the premises—namely, 1, 2, or 4. Of the three premises it does not seem very promising to deny 4 and claim that it is now in my power to bring it about that God has not believed the thing which in fact he has always believed. But both of the other premises are potentially vulnerable.

Suppose, for instance, we deny 1, the premise which says that it is now true that I will eat a cheese omelet tomorrow. This is not to say that I will not eat an omelet, but rather that it isn't now true either that I will eat one or that I won't eat one. I may, or I may not, and that's that. If someone conjectures, on the basis of my known addiction to cheese omelets, that "Hasker will have a cheese omelet tomorrow," then his conjecture may *come true* tomorrow morning, but it isn't true now. As of now, there just isn't any truth about what I will eat tomorrow.

It's important to be clear about the implications of this. It doesn't mean that God is not omniscient: Premise 2 of the argument is still accepted without question. But it does mean that there are quite a few matters with regard to the future (especially those concerning the free actions of persons) about which God does not, as yet, have any definite views, because there isn't, as yet, any truth to be known about these matters. As soon as there are such truths, God will be the first to know!

To many persons, this will seem to be a shocking and utterly unacceptable limitation on what God knows of the future. Still, it remains true that God knows everything; what he doesn't know doesn't exist to be known.[12] But there is another way out of the problem that historically has won much greater favor.

This way out has been found in the doctrine of *divine timelessness*. It should be said that this doctrine was not accepted only, and perhaps not even primarily, as a solution for the problem of foreknowledge. But the other reasons for the doctrine cannot be developed here; indeed the doctrine itself can be presented only in very sketchy terms. Our most usual way of conceiving God's eternity is to think of God as *everlasting:* God always has existed throughout infinite past time, and he always will exist. But according to a number of important theologians (including Augustine, Boethius, Anselm and Thomas Aquinas), this is really not correct. God's existence is not everlasting; it is timeless, outside of time altogether. Boethius defined eternity as "the complete and simultaneous possession of endless life." The key word is "simultaneous": God does not live his life moment by moment, as we do; rather he has it all at once, so that for him there is no past or future, but only a single, eternal, present moment—the "eternal now." It is vital to see that God's "present" is not *our* present moment: God's "now" is not identical with any moment of *our* time; rather it is outside of time altogether. A somewhat surprising but nevertheless accurate way of stating this is to say that God exists, but there is no time at which he exists, nor does he exist at all times.

How does this affect the problem of foreknowledge? If God is timeless, it will not be literally true to say that God knows things *before* they happen; rather he knows them timelessly. In the argument given above, the premise concerning God's omniscience will have to be modified as follows:

2'. It is impossible that God should believe anything false or fail to believe timelessly anything that is true.

From this, together with 1, we get:

3'. God timelessly believes that I will have a cheese omelet for breakfast tomorrow.

But in order to avoid the deterministic conclusion, we must affirm, instead of 4, that:

4'. It may sometimes be true that God timelessly believes a certain thing, and yet it is in my power to bring it about that God does not timelessly believe that thing.

Here we see the importance of the point that God's timeless present is not identical with any moment of our time. If God believes now, at the present time, that I will have an omelet, then it is already too late for me to do anything that would prevent God from having had that belief. But, to repeat this once more, God does *not* (according to the doctrine of timelessness) believe this, or anything else, *at the present time*. Rather, he believes things timelessly, entirely outside of our time sequence. And what it is that God timelessly believes depends, in part, on what I will freely choose to do tomorrow morning.

The doctrine of divine timelessness is surely a strange and difficult one, and many philosophers (including Christian philosophers) have claimed that it is incoherent, meaningless or self-contradictory. So far as I am able to tell this has not been shown; the alleged difficulties, insofar as they have been clearly stated, seem to be solvable. Nevertheless, the complexity and difficulty of this theory cannot be denied. Perhaps it would be wise for the reader neither to accept nor to reject the doctrine on the basis of the little that has been said about it here. But it does seem to provide a way, and perhaps the only way, to affirm consistently both that God has comprehensive knowledge of our future, and that we ourselves shall freely determine what (in certain respects) that future shall be.[13]

3

Minds
and
Bodies

A man or a woman is a physical thing like other physical things. A human body is heavy if one lifts it, solid yet yielding if one runs into it, capable of supporting weight if one leans against it. It consists of solids, liquids and gases, variously composed and mingled. It can be analyzed chemically or diagrammed geometrically. It has contours that can be photographed and smells that can be smelled. A human is, in short, a material object.

A man or woman is not a physical thing like other physical things. A sack of cement has weight but makes no weighty judgments; a wooden bench gives support but cannot be supportive. A running stream may be full of music, but it takes a human being to hear the music. A rock may be made into an altar, but it takes a living soul to worship at it. Humans, unlike other physical things, write poems and love letters, invent scientific theories and discover the depths of evil. They are like ordinary material objects, yet unlike them in so many ways.

The Mystery of Mind and Body

This, in a nutshell, is the mystery of mind and body. How is it that this familiar object, compounded out of ordinary chemicals, is yet able to transcend physical limitations and to live a life of the spirit? Or, to come at the mystery from the opposite direction, how does it happen that a rational spirit, capable of speculating about truth, beauty and goodness and of worshiping a Supreme Being, nevertheless finds itself embedded—some would say, imprisoned—in a body consisting of flesh and bone, blood and muscle? However one states the question, it remains a deep and perplexing mystery. And if anyone is ready with a quick and easy answer, it may be said with confidence that such a person has neither probed the depths of the question nor considered fully the complexities and difficulties that arise out of the proposed answer.

It may occur to you, however, that there is something wrong with the way in which the problem is being presented. If we compare a man or woman with a stone or a river, we may see little in common. But what of cows and horses, cats and canaries, lizards and turtles, fish and fireflies? Don't other living creatures present, as it were, a continuum of cases between humanity and inanimate nature? And mustn't these be considered if we are to put man in his proper place in the scheme of things?

The complaint is justified and will be discussed in due course. But considering the variety of living creatures does not by any means provide an easy resolution of the mystery of mind and body. Rather, it complicates the problem considerably. For one thing, there is the very real question as to how many of the "distinctive" characteristics of human beings are in fact shared by other creatures. Consider, for example, the controversies about the alleged linguistic abilities of apes. On the other hand, since some of the attributes which distinguish humans from ordinary material objects are shared by other creatures, some of the same questions will arise concerning those creatures as arise concerning human beings. If, for example, we think of a living organism as an assemblage of the microparticles of physics (electrons, quarks, gluons and the like), it seems a considerable mystery how such an assemblage of particles can experience a feeling such as pleasure or pain. Certainly our current physical theory, the best knowledge we have concerning the nature and behavior of these particles, gives us no help with this at all. And this remains true whether the organism in question is an amoeba (if amoebas have feelings), a fish, a snake, a leopard—or a human being.

I believe it is important to see at the outset that the mind-body relationship is deeply mysterious and will remain so whatever theory about it we finally adopt. That is to say, the mysteriousness is inherent in the subject matter and is not just the result of a confused or inadequate way of viewing it. If we do not see this, we may be apt to think we have found the correct answer when all we have really done is to point out difficulties in a rival theory. Thus one may feel that it is obviously absurd to suppose that a mere assemblage of atoms could compose symphonies or worship God —and, therefore, that the correct view must recognize the existence in man of an immaterial mind, soul or spirit. On the other hand, one may point to the numerous difficulties which arise if such an immaterial mind is postulated, and thus conclude that the correct view has to be some form of materialism.

Either of these conclusions might be correct, but as stated both are premature. This is so, first, because on this question (as with many other philosophical questions) there are not just two possible answers, such that by disproving one the other is automatically shown to be correct; and, second, because one is not justified in rejecting an opposing position because of its difficulties until one's own position has been carefully scrutinized and shown to be free from equal (or even greater) difficulties. But for this latter task, we absolutely need the help of philosophers who do not share our favored view, and who will therefore be both more acute and more zealous in finding flaws in it than we ourselves are likely to be.

At this point we need to begin to define more precisely both the mind-body problem and some of the key terms and concepts that are involved in the problem. One might think that the terms to begin with are "mind" and "body," but beginning this way would tend to imply that mind and body are both "things"—and this, as we shall see, is very much in controversy. It will be better, therefore, to begin by defining physical and mental *properties*. Let us say, then, that a *physical property* is a property or attribute which can characterize an ordinary physical object, whether or not that object is thought of as being alive or as being possessed of "mind," awareness or consciousness. Examples of physical properties would include such things as being seven feet three inches in diameter, weighing 127 pounds, being purple and smelling like Limburger cheese.

A *mental property,* on the other hand, is a property which can only characterize an entity which is possessed of some kind of consciousness or awareness. Examples would include feeling pain, seeing something blue, thinking to oneself that 12 is the square root of 144, and smelling something that smells like Limburger cheese. Given these definitions, we can state the mind-body problem as follows: *How are we to explain the fact—or what seems to be the fact—that the very same entities, in particular human beings, are characterized both by physical properties and by mental properties?*

Let me be quick to point out that these definitions are quite rough-and-ready and are by no means to be taken as the last word on the meanings of "mental" and "physical." In fact, there has been and continues to be a great deal of disagreement about the best way to define both of these terms. But the definitions given above, with the associated examples, suffice to point out a number of clear cases of mental and physical properties, and for present purposes this is all we really need. Let us proceed then to examine some of the answers to this most perplexing of problems.

Avoiding the Problem: Behaviorism and Idealism

In presenting the mind-body problem in the previous section, we have been assuming that there really are two fundamentally different kinds of properties which are possessed by human beings. If we accept this as a fact, then the task of explaining how and why it is a fact is a formidable one. But what if it is not a fact after all? What if one kind of property, when rightly understood, turns out to be simply a special case, a subclass, of the other kind of property? In this case the mind-body problem might be easily resolved or perhaps shown not to be a problem at all.

We shall now examine two philosophical theories which attempt this kind of resolution of the problem. *Philosophical behaviorism* states, in effect, that mental properties are really a special category of physical properties; they are, to be specific, *behavioral properties* of living organisms.[1] *Idealism,* on the other hand, holds that what we have termed physical properties are really properties of "ideas," thoughts or "sense data" which exist only in the minds of some person or persons. Either way, the mind-body problem is in effect eliminated by getting rid of one group of properties.

First, behaviorism, which may be stated as follows: *When we describe the mental states, attributes and actions of a person, we are really describing the person's behavior, and whatever can be said by talking about such mental properties can also be expressed by talking directly about behavior.* For example, there can be no doubt that Lucy (in the comic strip *Peanuts*) is very conceited. If we were asked what Lucy's conceit is, we should probably be inclined to say that it is a mental property of Lucy. It is a state of Lucy's mind, part of the way she thinks about herself. But if we were asked how we *know* that Lucy is conceited, we would have to point to her *behavior*—her actions in setting herself up as a "sidewalk psychiatrist," her constant disparagement of Charlie Brown and so on. Now, the behaviorist takes the apparently simple step of saying that this pattern of behavior just *is* Lucy's conceit. So, too, with

Charlie Brown's inferiority complex, Schroeder's love of music and the rest. In each case, the supposed mental attribute is really a highly complex pattern of behavior. Normally, to be sure, we don't trouble to spell out the behavior in detail; rather, we just say "Lucy is conceited" as a sort of shorthand for the whole complex pattern. But the point is that we *could* spell it out, and if we could not—if we had no idea how Lucy's "conceit" would translate into behavior—then there would be no sense in our assertion that she is conceited.

At least one further qualification must be added in order to protect behaviorism from obvious counterexamples. It sometimes happens that we think about something, have some feeling or make a decision without ever having the opportunity to express our thoughts in actual behavior. For example, I may have thought about what I would do in the event of an atomic attack, but if (as I devoutly hope) no such attack ever comes I may never do anything about it or even tell anyone about my thoughts. So, what is the behavior-statement equivalent to "Hasker has planned to do so-and-so in the case of an atomic attack"? In order to answer this and to handle many similar examples, the behaviorist speaks of actual *and potential* behavior; my plan means that *if there were an attack I would respond* in certain ways. Similarly, a full spelling out of Lucy's conceit would include statements about how Lucy *would respond* to this or that situation, even though many of these situations may never actually arise.

The arguments in support of behaviorism are complex and include many criticisms of other mind-body theories which cannot be gone into here. But one major benefit should be readily apparent from what has already been said: It eliminates the mind-body problem. The problem of why human beings have both mental and physical properties resolves itself into the question of why certain material objects, namely, human bodies, exhibit such complex and fascinating forms of behavior. To be sure, that question is not an easy one and may keep scientists busy for some little time, but their concerns as they wrestle with it need not include the mind-body problem.

The other view to be considered in this section, a view first clearly presented by Berkeley, is *idealism*. According to this view material objects, as we ordinarily think of them, have no real existence. "To be is to be perceived" was Berkeley's motto—the very existence of a tree, a stone, a building, *consists in* the fact that it is perceived, now by this mind, now by that one. The existence of such "sensible objects," as Berkeley called them, is thus entirely relative to the minds which perceive them.

Does this mean that, for example, if no one is looking at a tree, the tree ceases to exist, only to pop back into existence the moment someone else looks in its direction? Berkeley did not say this; what he said, rather, was that no tree ever *is* completely unobserved, for all that exists is continually present to the mind of God. God, furthermore, is also needed to *coordinate* the various perceptions which human beings have of the tree. If you observe a tree, for example, your perceptions are continually changing with the wind, the sunlight and so on. If I am viewing the same tree from the other side, then I am getting a different view of it, consistent with my position, the state of my eyesight, and so on. So what guarantees that we are seeing the same thing? There is no direct connection between the idea or image of the tree in my mind and the one in your mind. Nor is there (as we might ordinarily suppose) the tree "in itself," existing separately from both of us and operating as a common causal factor in our perceptions of it. What guarantees that when you see a tree I also see a tree, and indeed the very same tree? The answer, according to Berkeley, is that *God* guarantees this. He alone is able to give each of us the perceptions that we need to have, in order that we should all perceive the world as a single, unified and orderly whole. What better demonstration could there be of his power, wisdom and goodness? Berkeley in fact felt it to be a great merit of his theory that abolishing "material substance" made all things directly dependent on God and so put an end to materialism and atheism. But also, and not incidentally, idealism resolves the mind-body problem by making physical properties, as we have termed them, attributes of images or "ideas" which exist only as perceived by a mind.

So we have two opposite methods of resolving the mind-body problem: Behaviorism claims that the "ultimate constituents" of mental states and processes are bits of behavior, while idealism states that the ultimate constituents of physical objects such as trees, stones and skyscrapers are mental images, thoughts in the mind. Obviously both cannot be correct, but is either?

It is fair to say that most philosophers have now become convinced that behaviorism is not satisfactory as a philosophical theory of the mind. It is true that the connection between inner, mental experiences and overt behavior is both intimate and important, and the behaviorists deserve credit for calling attention to this fact and developing it through detailed analysis. But the further claim that mental experiences just *are* behavior does not seem to be justified, and attempts to show that our mental life can be completely described by talking only about behavior have run into seemingly insuperable difficulties. Only two points will be mentioned here.

First, some experiences by their very nature do not allow expression in overt behavior. Dreaming, for example, is by definition done while one is asleep; the actions "experienced" in the dream are never physically performed, nor can one narrate a dream while having it. The only behavior that can be fixed on as the expression of the dream is the dreamer's behavior of retelling the dream after awakening. But the dream itself, we think, happens during *sleep,* when there is no behavior at all. And what of dreams which are forgotten and never recalled?[2] But more fundamentally, is it not obvious that certain experiences (pain, elation, tasting pistachio ice cream and so on) contain elements which, whether or not they are *expressed in* behavior, are clearly *different from* overt behavior of any kind? These "raw feels," as they have been called, seem to be an insurmountable problem for a behavioristic philosophy of mind.

But what of idealism? About this I will say here only two things. First, it is very difficult, if not impossible, to give a direct refutation of idealism—to show that it is logically inconsistent or contradicts established facts. But, second, in spite of this the theory seems immensely implausible; it runs so much against the grain of our normal beliefs about the world that only a really overwhelming case in its favor could make us accept it. A bit more will be said about it in the next chapter. In the meantime, let us turn to some solutions which begin by accepting the real existence of the physical body.

Dualism

By all odds the most influential mind-body theory in Western civilization has been mind-body *dualism*. Dualism was first developed as a philosophical theory by some of the Greek philosophers, notably Plato. It was adopted by most of the Christian thinkers of the first few centuries and subsequently came to share Christianity's dominance of European civilization. In recent times it has been placed somewhat in the shadow, but it continues to be the working viewpoint of large numbers of people and as such demands serious consideration. The version of dualism discussed here is that of Descartes, by far the most influential dualist of modern times, but much of what is said applies to other forms of dualism as well.

Dualism begins by taking quite seriously the fact that human beings have both physical properties and mental properties—as opposed to theories like idealism and behaviorism which collapse the two types of properties into one. Furthermore, dualism gives a clear and straightforward explanation of the existence of the two types of properties: physical properties, it says, are properties of the body, while mental properties are properties of the mind.

(Dualists sometimes use the word "soul" instead of "mind"; according to dualism the two words refer to the same thing.) The body is an ordinary physical thing, following the same laws which govern nature in general, but it has no mental properties, no awareness of any kind. Even a simple sensation, such as the pain felt when you scratch your finger, is not a property of the body but rather of the mind as influenced by the body.

The mind, on the other hand, has mental properties but no physical properties—it thinks, perceives and imagines but has no size, shape, mass, or even any spatial location. A person's mind and her body, then, are about as different from each other as any two things could be—yet they are not disconnected; on the contrary, they are continually interacting with each other. For this reason, the full name of the theory is *dualistic interactionism*.

Whenever you have some sensory experience, such as stubbing your toe or seeing a traffic light, the sensory information, after being processed in the necessary ways by your brain, is "picked up" by your mind, and this is when you experience the stub or the red light. And whenever you decide to do anything, the decision, which occurs in your mind, is transmitted via the brain to the various muscles which carry out the decision. In fact, one can conceive of the mind-brain relationship as being like that between a computer operator and her computer. The brain is the "central computer" for the body, receiving information from the various sense organs and sending out instructions through the nervous system. The mind, as the operator, "reads out" information from the brain and decides on the course of action to be followed, which is then "typed into" the brain's computer console and carried out by the appropriate parts of the body. Of course one must not think of the "operator" as *physically present* within the brain: The mind is completely nonphysical and is not literally located anywhere at all; but it does *operate* on the brain in such a way as to affect brain function and therefore bodily behavior.

Further points of interest concern the origin and destiny of the mind. Since the mind is seen as a completely nonphysical entity, the mind (or soul) cannot be generated through the biological process of reproduction. Instead, many dualists have held that each human person is endowed with a soul which is directly and individually created by God. And since the soul is nonphysical, there is no reason why its existence should be threatened by the death of its body. So dualism lends itself very readily to a belief in life after death. Christian theologians typically have held that the soul will be *re-embodied* in a changed, resurrection body; this view is consistent with mind-body dualism but is not required by it.

Many of the advantages of dualism are implicit in what has already been said. It recognizes the existence of both physical and mental properties of human beings, and it explains this fact in a straightforward way. It allows full scope for the scientific study of nature. (Descartes, the originator of dualism in the form here described, was deeply involved in the development of early modern physics.) At the same time, it recognizes the existence of an immaterial or "spiritual" part of man, so that certain aspects of human life (for example, morality and religion) cannot be fully comprehended by scientific study alone. It thus lends itself better than many other views to an affirmation of free will, although it does not require this. On the whole, dualism seems to harmonize quite well with a religious, specifically with a Christian, world view.

The most frequent objection to dualism proceeds by attacking the assertion of mind-body interaction which is central to the theory. Once we have conceived of mind and body as two entirely different types of reality, how is it possible for there to be the intimate and continuous cause-effect interaction required by dualism? How can the mind, totally lacking as it is said to be in any kind of physical reality, nevertheless bring about physical changes within the brain? And of course such changes, were they to occur, would come about in defiance of the laws of physics, which presumably govern physical processes in the brain as well as elsewhere.

There is much less in this objection than is generally thought. To begin with, *of course* the dualist will affirm that the physical processes within the brain are not completely predictable by physical law; the laws of physics describe the behavior of particles and the like *when no nonphysical influence* (such as that of the mind) *is acting upon them*. It may be true that there is some difficulty in imagining just how this influence operates, but what of that? There is no reason to think that reality is limited by what is easy for us to imagine. If it could be proved, from premises which are evidently true, that mind-body interaction is impossible, then the dualist would be in trouble. But no such proof has been given.[3]

But there are other difficulties with dualism that are not so easily brushed aside. For one thing, dualism, in spite of its affirmation of mind-body interaction, is hard pressed to explain the *extent* of the mind's dependence on the body as we actually find it. From the standpoint of dualism, it is readily understandable that physical damage to the brain or nervous system should interrupt the flow of sensory information from the body, as well as the mind's ability to initiate bodily actions. But why should *consciousness itself* be interrupted by a blow on the head or by the action of drugs? And how does dualism account for the profound changes of personality and character which may result either from physical damage to the brain or from chemical imbalances within it?[4] It seems likely that any adequate account of these phenomena will have to recognize that the mind is dependent upon the brain in a way that is more fundamental than dualism is willing to allow.

Another group of objections to dualism arises from the intriguing yet baffling problem of the souls of animals. Do animals have souls or don't they? Descartes, impressed with the difficulties which arise if we attribute souls to animals, decided that they do not. This means that animals are purely physical automata, with physiological reactions but no actual feelings, sensations or experiences of any kind. When your dog jumps up to greet you as you come home, or yelps when you step on his tail, it may seem to you that the dog really is feeling joy or pain, but nothing of the sort is true. What you observe is entirely the result of automatic physiological reactions within the dog's body. But clearly this is absurd! In order to avoid the absurdity, the dualist must affirm that animals do indeed have souls—not, to be sure, souls just like those of human beings, but souls all the same.

This, however, opens the way to further problems. Where do all these souls come from? It may seem not unreasonable that God should individually create a soul for each human being, but do we want to say this also about rabbits, toads and termites? And what happens to the souls of animals when the organisms perish? Are they also, like human souls, naturally immortal? If not, why not? And what of those organisms, like starfish, which can be cut into parts with each part subsequently developing into a complete organism? Before such a division there is one starfish and therefore one soul. Afterward, there are two starfish and, presumably, two souls. Where did the second soul come from? For the dualist, no good answer seems available.[5]

These are not, I think, merely frivolous objections. Rather they point to a serious difficulty with dualism. The dualistic view draws, and is intended to draw, a very strong contrast between man as a spiritual being and "mere" physical nature. But the gulf thus fixed between matter and spirit means that the entire living creation other than man is left unprovided for—and it may be that this can only be rectified by abandoning or fundamentally modifying dualism.

Materialism

Man is a wholly material being: This is the central thesis of *materialism*. Materialism, like dualism, comes in several varieties; currently the most popular variety is the *mind-body identity theory*. This theory does not deny that humans have both mental and physical attributes but says that both are attributes of the same thing—namely, the living human organism. A human being *is* his body, and the body is the person.

Another way to look at materialism is this: In discussing dualism, we said that the brain can be likened to the central control computer of the body, and the mind to its operator. But does every computer need an operator? We are familiar in fiction, if not yet in everyday life, with computers that "set up on their own" and operate independently of human control. Think, for example, of Hal, the psychotic computer in *2001: A Space Odyssey*. For the materialist, the human brain is a self-operating computer. The thoughts and other mental properties of humans are simply properties of complex, highly organized physical systems—namely, human brains. Whether manmade computers will ever be able really to *think*—as opposed to *simulating* thought processes— may be an open question: Does consciousness exist only in biological systems, such as humans and other animals, or would it also arise in a properly constructed assemblage of microchips and integrated circuits? But whether or not ordinary computers can think, the "meat computer" which each of us carries around in his or her head can and does.

One merit of materialism is its simplicity. Instead of explaining human life in terms of an immaterial mind whose nature is obscure and whose very existence is controversial, it limits itself to the familiar material organism whose existence is indisputable and whose characteristics are readily amenable to scientific study. In fact, the desire to have a thoroughly scientific understanding of human nature is one of the strongest motivations for adopting materialism. The dualist's immaterial mind is seen, rightly, as a barrier that would prevent us from fully integrating human life and activity into a unified scientific perspective in which the laws of physical science are the fundamental operating principles of the universe. The phenomenal success of science to date makes such a unified perspective a reasonable hope, and materialism is the mind-body theory which best accords with this hope. It should also be pointed out that materialism is completely free from the objections noted against dualism: All the objections result from the gulf between mind and matter, and materialism never allows that gulf to open in the first place.

But on further consideration the advantages of materialism may seem less clear. Materialism is simpler in that it has one basic type of substance instead of two, but there remains the duality of physical and mental *properties*. Materialists have tried in various ways to eliminate distinctively mental properties, but none of these attempts seems to be very successful. And it is not clear that the elimination of mental substance represents a real gain in simplicity if we must then ascribe to the physical substance properties quite unlike those it is known to have in all other contexts. Explaining how consciousness, feeling and other mental attributes arise from combinations of physical particles may not be a great deal easier than explaining the origin and nature of the immaterial mind.

Materialism's claim to produce a complete scientific understanding of human nature is also open to question. It has to be emphasized that such an understanding does not now exist; scientific progress has indeed been remarkable and must not be ignored, but it is by no means clear that it is leading in the direction of a single "unified science" in which all human thought and behavior is explained in physicalistic terms. And the tenability of this objective is called into question by some of the arguments presented in the chapter "Freedom and Necessity": It was argued there that physical determinism (with or without a random element due to quantum indeterminacy) entails not only the denial of moral responsibility but also the denial of human rationality—a consequence which is clearly unacceptable to the materialist, who relies heavily on scientific knowledge. Unless this argument can be met, the materialist will be forced to admit that there is after all something about human beings which cannot be captured in explanations couched in terms of the physical sciences.

It would seem that the disagreement between the dualist and the materialist, like that between the determinist and the libertarian, is connected with deep-rooted motivations which do not easily yield to philosophical argument. Persons who are deeply committed to a scientific world view may acknowledge the difficulties of materialism but will tend to cling to it anyway as they work for solutions of the difficulties. Similarly, persons committed to a religious and humanistic world view will continue to affirm at least some of the tenets of dualism in spite of their recognition of the difficulties of that viewpoint. One's views on the mind-body problem will tend to be strongly influenced by one's general perspective on the way things are. But the converse is true as well: surely one of the acid tests for a world view is whether it is able to provide a consistent, coherent and acceptable account of the nature of humanity. Both materialism and dualism seem to leave something to be desired in this regard.

Emergentism
There is no logical limit to the number of sections in this chapter. Unlike the free-will controversy, the mind-body problem does not divide up into a limited number of clear-cut, mutually exclusive alternatives. But of the many additional views which could be considered, only one more will be pursued here. Is it possible, we may ask, to develop a mind-body theory which will combine some of the advantages of both dualism and materialism while avoiding many of the disadvantages of each?

The difficulties of dualism arise from the gulf which is created between mind and matter when we assert that mind is a separate element added to the physical organism "from outside." Materialism, on the other hand, reduces man entirely to a physical organism functioning according to natural laws, with the result that crucial aspects of human existence—morality, rationality, aesthetic experience, religion—inevitably are either slighted or denied altogether. What seems to be needed, then, is a view in which the human mind or soul is *grounded in* the human biological organism without being *reduced to* that organism.

Suppose we say, first of all, that *the human mind or soul is produced by the human brain and is not a separate element added to the brain from outside.* This of course agrees with materialism, but the difference from materialism is apparent when we add that while the mind is produced by the brain and dependent upon it, *nevertheless the mind is distinct from the brain and its activities are not completely explainable in terms of brain function.* This statement, in contrast with the first one given, indicates the element of truth in dualism which is denied by materialism.

But how can we conceive of the mind-body relationship in accordance with these two statements? Here a helpful analogy may be found in the theory of fields in the physical sciences—the magnetic field and the gravitational field, for example. In both of these cases the field is certainly *produced by* a generating physical object, but it is also clear that the field is *distinct from* the object, as is shown by the fact that the object is sharply localized whereas the field spreads out for an indefinite distance in all directions. So, we may surmise, the "field of consciousness" or "soul-field" is generated by the appropriately complex organic functioning of the human brain. And just as the fields of physics continually interact with the generating body (as in an electric motor or generator), so the "conscious field" continually interacts with its own generating organism. Of course the distinguishing characteristics of human beings are not exemplified by the fields of physics. What we can say, however, is this: Just as electrical, magnetic and gravitational fields function in accordance with the laws of their respective natures, so the soul-field functions in accordance with its own inherent natural potentialities, which include, among other things, both rational autonomy and moral freedom. This view may be termed *emergentism,* in recognition of the appearance or "emergence" of the soul-field as a result of the organization and functioning of the brain and nervous system.

To make this clearer, certain questions need to be answered. What exactly is this field supposed to be? Is it a *thing*—or, as philosophers say, a *substance*? The answer is that the conscious field is to be thought of as a concrete, individual, continuing entity, and thus a substance in at least one sense of that term. Is the soul-field a "mental substance," like the mind or soul of dualism? It is certainly mental in that it is characterized by mental properties such as feeling, choosing and imagining, but it does not share other characteristics of the dualist's mental substance. The soul-field has spatial location and extension, and it is also physically divisible; under certain circumstances dividing an organism into parts may result in the division of the associated conscious field. The gulf between mental and physical simply is not as wide for emergentism as it is for dualism; that is a principal difference between the views. But isn't emergentism, after all, a kind of dualism? Perhaps in a sense it is, but it is sufficiently different from the common types of dualism (for instance, the theories of René Descartes and Thomas Aquinas) that it is useful to designate it by a name of its own.

A theory of this kind, while certainly not proven by scientific data, seems to be entirely consistent with all scientific findings to date. And it clearly avoids the major disadvantages noted in the other theories. Unlike materialism, it avoids simply equating a person with her body, and it recognizes the distinctive aspects of human functioning which are negated if it is claimed that human activity is entirely explainable in terms of physics and chemistry. Like dualism, it affirms interaction between a person's mind and her body, but such interaction is far more credible and intelligible if it is interaction between a field and its generating body than if it is interaction between two substances which are entirely diverse in their nature and origin. And emergentism readily accepts the multiple dependencies of the mind on the biological functioning of the brain and nervous system; for emergentism (unlike dualism) this is what would naturally be expected. Furthermore, the problem about the souls of animals is on this view a nonproblem: *Of course* the beasts have souls, but souls that are less complex and developed than those of human beings because they are generated by less complex and less developed nervous systems.

But what of life after death? We have not attempted to give a philosophical proof of a future life and perhaps could not do so. It is clear, however, that this is a crucial issue for many persons (including Christians!), one which cannot be ignored in assessing mind-body theories. Does emergentism, with its assertion that the mind or soul is generated and sustained in being by the biological organism, imply also that the soul will perish along with the body? If it does imply this, that would constitute a serious objection to the theory.

But emergentism need not be taken to imply the soul's mortality. The analogy with the magnetic field may suggest that the field should disappear along with the generating body. But this may not be invariably true even of the fields of physics. A black hole, for example, is an incredibly intense gravitational field which is originally generated by a massive object. But once it has formed, it literally squeezes the generating object out of existence. Thus, according to Roger Penrose, "After the body has collapsed in, it is better to think of the black hole as a self-sustaining gravitational field in its own right. It has no further use for the body which originally built it!"[6] Could the human mind then, like a black hole, become a *self-sustaining* field of consciousness?

Another possibility, perhaps of more interest to Christians, is suggested by the neurologist Wilder Penfield. He hypothesizes that throughout life the mind is supplied with energy by the brain, but, he says, "Whether there is such a thing as communication between man and God and whether energy can come to the mind of man from an outside source after his death is for each individual to decide for himself. Science has no such answers."[7]

To sum up this point: Emergentism does not guarantee the immortality of the soul; but it is consistent with the affirmation of life after death for human beings if evidence for a future life can be provided from another quarter. And surely this is sufficient. It should be enough for us if we are able, philosophically, to conceive the possibility of eternal life; it must be left to God to demonstrate the reality.

So much for the strengths of emergentism; what are its weaknesses? Since this view has not yet been subjected to the same sort of intensive investigation and criticism as have dualism and materialism, it may be premature to try to answer the question. It is clear that insofar as emergentism is in many respects positioned between dualism and materialism, it is open to attacks from both directions. Thus, some dualists will view emergentism as a thinly disguised materialism, and some materialists will regard it as merely a minor variant of dualism. The emergentist does share with the materialist the belief that mind and consciousness result from the functioning of the physical organism, and therefore also the difficulty of explaining how this is possible. To this the emergentist, if he or she is a Christian, may respond by citing the biblical testimony that man was created from the dust of the earth—dust which, itself the creation of the all-wise God, is rich with potential beyond our imagining. Whatever view we accept, there is plenty of mystery left.[8]

Eternal Life: Immortality or Resurrection?
In the preceding sections we have implied that dualism is likely to be acceptable to religious believers because it implies the existence (or at least the possibility) of life after death, whereas materialism will be unacceptable because it denies this. A number of Christian thinkers, however, would find this emphasis misconceived. Dualism, they would say, does indeed offer support for the doctrine of the *immortality of the soul,* but this doctrine is not essential to Christianity and may not even be compatible with good Christian theology.

The belief in immortality, originating in Greek thought, is tied to such dubious notions as that the soul is inherently divine or quasi-divine and that the body is evil, a prison in which the soul is confined until its blessed liberation by death. In contrast to this is the Hebrew, and biblical, belief in the *resurrection of the body:* It is not that our "souls" survive, but that God on the day of judgment resurrects the *entire person* for a life either of blessedness or of damnation. Thus the dualist's belief in a separable soul is at best irrelevant and at worst may represent a damaging intrusion of pagan philosophical concepts into the Christian faith.

Much of this can be dealt with summarily here. It is true that some dualists have believed in the inherent divinity of the soul and the inherent evil of the body, as well as in the superiority of a disembodied existence. But none of these notions are implied by the core conception of dualism as elaborated here, and Christian theologians who are dualists have generally managed to avoid these problematic notions. Thus according to Thomas Aquinas a human being is a composite substance consisting of both soul and body. The disembodied soul, in between death and resurrection, exists in a state of incompleteness, which will be remedied only when God raises us on the last day. While Aquinas does draw heavily upon Greek philosophical conceptions, it is hard to see what in his thought on these matters could be viewed as a betrayal of the Christian conception of human beings.

There remains, however, an interesting philosophical question: Is belief in a separable soul necessary for the doctrine of eternal life? According to one group of philosophers, who may be termed "Christian materialists," the answer is no.[9] There is no need of a soul to provide the link of identity between the person who dies and the same person resurrected; the truth is rather that the *entire person* perishes at death—ceases entirely to exist—and then is *re-created* by God in the resurrection. But, one might ask, is this really possible? Would a person, just like me, created after I have died, really be me? Or would it be a mere replica, a simulation of me? In order to answer such questions, John Hick proposes a couple of test cases:

> Suppose, first, that someone—John Smith—living in the USA
> were suddenly and inexplicably to disappear from before the
> eyes of his friends, and that at the same moment an exact rep-
> lica of him were inexplicably to appear in India. . . . Further,
> the "John Smith" replica thinks of himself as being the John
> Smith who disappeared in the USA. After all possible tests
> have been made and have proved positive, the factors leading
> his friends to accept "John Smith" as John Smith would surely
> prevail and would cause them to overlook even his mysterious
> transference from one continent to another, rather than treat
> "John Smith," with all John Smith's memories and other char-
> acteristics, as someone other than John Smith.

> Suppose, second, that our John Smith, instead of inexpli-
> cably disappearing, dies, but that at the moment of his death a
> "John Smith" replica, again complete with memories and all
> other characteristics, appears in India. Even with the corpse on
> our hands we would, I think, still have to accept this "John
> Smith" as the John Smith who died. We would have to say that
> he had been miraculously re-created in another place.[10]

An initial response to this might be that while Hick's examples
are somewhat plausible, this plausibility is due to reasons which
have nothing to do with the case he is trying to make. In order to
support Hick's case, the examples must be seen as instances of
total personal annihilation followed by re-creation. But to a generation of *Star Trek* fans the first example suggests merely an advanced form of transportation: It occurs to us that Smith's re-
appearance should have occurred in the transporter room of the
Enterprise! The second example, of course, excludes this interpretation. But I would suggest that all of us, even if we are not pro-
fessed dualists, have a strong tendency to read the example as
though Smith's *mind,* or *soul,* having survived his physical death,
is re-embodied in the newly created body. (Hick is, I think, correct in assuming that it doesn't matter that it is not Smith's *origi-*

nal body which is resurrected. Surely God's ability to raise us from the dead can't be thought to depend on whether enough quarks, electrons and so on from our original bodies are available to make the resurrection bodies. For that matter, are resurrection bodies composed of ordinary physical "stuff"?)

Hick will insist, however, that the second example is to be read without the assumption of a soul which survives—that Smith has undergone total personal annihilation and has then been re-created. But is this intelligible? What exactly, according to Hick's view, is a human being supposed to be? One possibility is that "John Smith" names a *general category* of some kind, so that there can be any number of John Smith's so long as they are sufficiently similar in relevant respects. If this is correct, then there is no problem in saying that the "John Smith" replica really is John Smith. In fact there is no logical reason (though there might be other kinds of reasons) why God must wait until Smith is dead to re-create him—there could be any number of John Smiths alive at the same time, and all of them would have equal claim to being considered the real John Smith. And this leads to some interesting questions: If Smith is married, which of the numerous replicas is Mrs. Smith's husband? And who would be responsible for the parking ticket he got last month?

The obvious alternative to this view—and the one which, I think, Hick and other Christian materialists are really bound to accept—is that John Smith is identical with a certain living human body. But if we apply this to Hick's second example, then the conclusion we come to is that John Smith no longer exists. Smith's *body* exists, all right, but the body is dead; and therefore so is he. The replica body is alive, but this can't be the body that is identical with John Smith, for *that* body is stretched out cold and dead on the floor. So the replica is an imposter, a new person remarkably similar to John Smith.

If this is correct, then we are led to the conclusion that materialism really is logically incompatible with life after death. To say this does not in any way deny or minimize the omnipotence of God. The question is not how much power God has but whether the act that is attributed to God is logically consistent. It has long been recognized that divine omnipotence does not include the power to perform contradictory acts, such as creating a square circle or bringing it about that $2 + 2 = 17$. If the argument given here is correct, it is equally nonsensical to assert that God creates out of nothing a person that has already lived, died and completely passed out of existence. So it *is* essential, if we are going to affirm eternal life, that we should hold that in some way the "core person" survives bodily death and continues in existence. And this is just what is offered, in their different ways, by both dualism and emergentism.

4
The World

*L*ike man himself, the world in which man lives is filled with mystery. Most of the time, to be sure, we are engaged with the world around us in a practical way —making a living from it, escaping its dangers and shaping it to our needs and convenience. But there are moments in which these practical concerns can be put aside, and in those moments, if we are at all sensitive, we are apt to be seized with curiosity, admiration and wonder. Some of our curiosity is satisfied by science, but there is always more to be known. And at least some people sense an underlying meaning in things which science not only cannot exhaust but cannot even begin to grasp. Tennyson expressed this when he wrote:

Flower in the crannied wall,
I pluck you out of the crannies,
I hold you here, root and all, in my hand,
Little flower—but *if* I could understand

What you are, root and all, and all in all,
I should know what God and man is.[1]

Here Tennyson seems to glimpse, in a fragmentary way, some sort of "grand design," some overall scheme of things of which the flower is a part and to which, had we but the eyes, mind and heart to see, it might provide a vital clue. Was he right about this? It is difficult to say; the metaphysics of flowers seems to be a somewhat neglected topic.

What Is the Real Nature of the World?

Whether or not a proper metaphysical understanding of the natural world will end in such a grand vision as Tennyson suggests, there is no doubt where it must begin. Any approach to these topics has to start with the data we actually have, our daily commerce with such ordinary things as trees and dirt, shrubs and flowers, insects and animals. Nor should we neglect buildings and bridges and machines and scientific instruments; all of these, while manmade and thus "artificial," are instances of natural materials and natural forces. It is concerning these ordinary sorts of things that we speak when we ask, What is the *real nature* of the world?

But, you may wonder, what question is there that is not already answered by our daily experience and use of these things? A pine tree, for example, has dark green needles, rough brownish bark, and a fresh, penetrating scent. More could be learned by closer observation, and still more by scientific study of the tree. Beyond this, what is the problem?

This is a very reasonable, common-sensical response. And it contains within itself the germ, the leading idea, of a definite philosophical position on our topic. The theory of *common-sense realism* (also sometimes called "naive realism") holds that *physical objects really exist and really have the properties that we perceive them to have*. Thus the pine tree *really is* green and brown, rough textured, fragrant and so on, just as we experience it to be.

Still, you may ask, what is all the fuss about? What, after all, *could* the pine tree be if not green, rough, fragrant and the like? And why dignify the claim that it really is these things by calling it a metaphysical theory? Aren't we just inventing a problem where no problem exists?

Actually there *is* a problem, and seeing it is the first step toward comprehending the topics to be discussed in this chapter. Consider, first of all, the claim that ordinary physical objects really have the properties that we perceive them to have. Just what are those properties? The tree's needles, we say, are green; but in red light they will be nearly black, and in very dim light things have hardly any color at all. Also, of course, there are persons who suffer from red-green colorblindness. Since they can't distinguish colors which to the rest of us are strikingly different, they can't be seeing those colors as we do. Similar observations will apply to senses other than vision. So once again, what *are* the properties which, according to common-sense realism, ordinary objects really possess?

This question is not too difficult for the realist to answer. While acknowledging that objects will *appear to have* different characteristics under different conditions (without the objects themselves undergoing actual change), he will simply state that objects *really have* the properties that are perceived under *normal conditions* and by *normal observers.* Thus a tree is green if it is seen to be green by a person with normal color vision in conditions of adequate lighting with "white" light, that is, light the color of sunlight. A room is warm if it is so experienced by persons in good health, as opposed to those suffering from chills or fever. And similarly for the other senses.

This answer seems adequate as far as it goes. It needs to be pointed out, however, that the realist's "normal observers" are in fact normal *human* observers. But what about nonhuman observers? It's pretty clear that animals don't all perceive the world as we do: Dogs, for example, have poor vision at a distance and little or no color vision. In this case we may feel secure in saying that it is we who perceive the world "as it really is." But what if human sight is compared to that of an eagle? And what of the sense of smell, which for most other mammals is far richer, more complex and more informative than it is for humans?

We might perhaps be tempted to claim that our superior intelligence makes us the authority on how things "really" are. But what if we were to encounter extraterrestrial intelligences? It seems entirely possible (to some of us, even overwhelmingly likely) that there are other intelligent creatures "out there." If there are, there is no reason to think they will experience the world exactly as we do. To take a very mild example: In one of Robert Heinlein's novels, the human visitors to Mars are unable to appreciate Martian painting because the Martians exploit a range of colors in the infrared portion of the spectrum which are invisible to human eyes. Far more radical deviations can be imagined, including senses entirely different from those enjoyed by humans (consider the use of sonar by bats and dolphins). So we and the E.T.s simply will not agree about how things appear or are perceived, and it is hard to justify saying that one group is right and the other wrong. The obvious answer would seem to be that we describe how things really are *for us,* and the E.T.s describe how things are *for them.* But this answer would be upsetting to the common-sense realists (of both species), holding as they do that things really are *in themselves* as they appear to us.

It is not my intention at this point to decide whether common-sense realism is right or wrong; the point is simply to see that there are serious questions about this position, questions which demand further discussion. In order to carry on this discussion, we need to further clarify our terminology.

The term "realism" is used in metaphysics for a number of different positions, all of which affirm the *real existence* (also called the "independent" existence) of something whose reality has been denied or questioned. It should be noted that common-sense realism, as defined above, involves two distinct assertions about physical objects: (1) that they really exist, and (2) that they really have the properties we perceive them to have. It would seem possible for someone to affirm the first of these assertions while remaining uncommitted with regard to the second. Let us then define *realism concerning physical objects* (often referred to simply as "realism") as the view that *physical objects really exist and their existence does not depend on there being minds to perceive them.* Common-sense realism will thus be one variety of realism concerning physical objects; as we shall see, there are other varieties.

One kind of realism which must be clearly distinguished from the uses of "realism" in this chapter is *realism concerning universals,* which affirms that such things as properties and attributes really exist "on their own," separate both from the objects which exemplify them and from the minds which apprehend them. Beauty, for example, exists independently both of beautiful things and of the minds which enjoy them. Realism concerning universals is one of the many important metaphysical topics not covered in this book.

The Idealist Rejection of Realism

One position which sharply rejects common-sense realism is *idealism,* already encountered in the previous chapter. According to idealism, the existence of objects such as trees, bridges and flycatchers *consists in* the fact that these things are perceived by various minds—human minds and also the mind of God. Idealism thus does not deny the *existence* of ordinary objects—idealists are well aware that there are such things as trees—but it denies their *independent* existence by making them simply aspects of human (and possibly divine) perceptual experience.

Some people may find it difficult to take idealism seriously as a theory about the real nature of the world. The problem is that idealism runs so strongly counter to our normal ways of regarding our world that it would take extremely powerful arguments to overcome this and induce us to consider it favorably. Berkeley, to be sure, thought that he had given such arguments, but on close examination his reasoning does not seem to be especially compelling.[2] Berkeley, however, would also have contested my claim that his theory runs against the grain of our natural beliefs about the world. The ordinary person, he argued, believes in the reality of perceptible objects insofar as he can see them, hear them, feel them and so on. In other words, the reality of these objects concerns him *insofar as the objects are perceptible to the senses* —and *this* reality is fully endorsed by idealism. It is only a few philosophers who, tangled in a web of meaningless abstractions, have convinced themselves that there must be something *more* to trees and flowers than the fact that they are perceived. Berkeley wished to point out to them that they had no reasons for this position and that, in fact, the very sentences in which they expressed their view were lacking in any definite meaning. Thus enlightened, these philosophers might be induced to rejoin the rest of the human race in recognizing that the "reality" of things which is important to us is their reality *as sensible objects:* Their "being" just *is* their being perceived.

It seems clear, however, that Berkeley's theory conflicts with our ordinary view of things. It is quite true that we become convinced of the reality of physical objects primarily because they impress themselves on our senses. But it is undeniably part of our bedrock conviction about the world that when several persons are observing some object—say, a mountain—then they are all perceiving *the very same object.* They may perceive it differently for various reasons (position, level of attention, variations in eyesight and so on), but there is *a single thing* which they are all perceiving. Idealism denies this: The various "ideas" or sense impressions in the minds of the different observers are entirely independent of each other, and only their constant coordination by God enables us all to see (approximately) the same thing. This might conceivably be the truth about the world, but it is certainly not the way we ordinarily suppose things to be.

So idealism is a position which seems to be somewhat lacking in terms of inherent plausibility. Nevertheless, it will be profitable to evaluate idealism using the criteria of adequacy for metaphysical theories developed in chapter one. Do these criteria show idealism to be less adequate than realism? If so, how?

The requirement of *logical consistency* seems to be satisfied by idealism; a carefully formulated idealistic theory need not involve any self-contradictions. Nor is idealism easily shown to be lacking in *factual adequacy*. For what facts could be in disagreement with idealism? If the facts in question consist in some kind of sensory experience, then idealism will welcome them with open arms. And if they do not consist in sensory experience, the idealist can contest them, refuse to accept them as "facts." On the criterion of factual adequacy, the idealist's position is invulnerable.

When it comes to *explanatory adequacy,* however, the situation is much different. Consider again the situation of several people observing the same mountain over a period of time. According to realism, there is a *single object* which they are all perceiving—namely, the mountain—and it is this single object which, impinging on the sense organs of the various observers, causes them to have the perceptions they do have. Some changes in the perceptions are caused by changes in the mountain itself: There is an avalanche, or the summit is obscured by clouds. Other changes in perceptions are caused by changes in the observers: They look away, they become tired and go to sleep, their eyes become fatigued and unable to focus, and so on.

Now compare this with the same situation as described by idealism. On this view there is no physically existing mountain, nor do the observers have any physical sense organs. When there is an avalanche, it is God himself who brings this about by adjusting each individual observer's perception *as if* an avalanche were occurring. When an observer becomes weary, God adjusts that observer's perceptions *as if* her eyes were fatigued and incapable of focusing correctly. And so on.

Is it not evident that the explanation offered by realism is superior? Not everyone would agree to the existence of God, as required by idealism. But even assuming that God exists, why should he bring about our experiences by such a contrived and artificial method as is postulated by idealism? Instead of so meticulously manipulating our perceptions *as if* they were the result of independently existing physical objects, why didn't God just create the objects themselves and have done with it? The hypothesis of realism (supplemented by scientific investigation) promises to account for the perceptions with both their accuracies and their inaccuracies in terms of a unified, coherent conceptual scheme, while the idealist is reduced to saying of each individual perception merely that it is so because God decided that it should be so.

The Scientific Critique of Realism

Idealism rejects realism outright, but modern science also creates problems for realism in a more subtle way. Specifically, science seems to conflict with common-sense realism. It may seem strange that there should be such a conflict. Science is, after all, devoted to the study of presumably real physical objects, and its conclusions about those objects depend entirely on verification through sense perception. How then can science question the reality of the very objects which constitute both its evidential base and its subject matter?

The difficulty arises from the fact that the description of physical objects by science is very different from that given by common sense based on perception. Take, for example, a pebble, a "simple" piece of rock; to perception and common sense, a straightforward and unremarkable object. But scientists have discovered—or hypothesized—in the pebble a whole host of complex, arcane and unobservable objects, properties and relationships, from the "atoms" of ancient Epicureanism to the electrons and protons, strong and weak nuclear forces, quarks and gluons of the most recent science. Furthermore, scientific thought shows an unmistakable tendency to *replace* the pebble, and other ordinary objects, with constructs made up of the theoretical entities mentioned and others like them.

The best-known (though by no means the first) statement of this view comes from Locke. According to him, objects have certain "primary qualities," such as spatial location, mass and motion, which really belong to the objects *in themselves,* but also "secondary qualities" such as color, sound, taste, smell and warmth or coolness which do not exist in the objects themselves but *only in the minds which perceive them.* Thus for Locke pebbles and primroses really exist, separate from our minds (he is, therefore, a realist), but they exist stripped, as it were, of many of the qualities that make them interesting, valuable and important to us. The *perceived* flower is colorful, fragrant and deliciously cool to the touch, but the *real* flower is none of these things. A bleak outlook on the world, indeed! And Locke's reason for this view is quite clear. The primary qualities alone really exist in the physical objects, because these are the qualities needed by science for its explanations. (Locke was well aware that the primary qualities of physical objects would include properties of their "minute parts" or, as we would say, their atoms, electrons and so on. But the science of his day [the late seventeenth century] could tell him little in detail about this.)

It may occur to you, however, that science is being taken a bit too literally. Science and its theories are all very well, you may say, but why should we allow the scientific description of the world, which no doubt is quite in order in its place and for its special purpose, to take over and replace our common-sense view of things? Surely there must be a way to give science its due, to acknowledge its success in predicting and controlling nature, without making it the arbiter of ultimate reality? There is indeed a way to do this; the approach suggested in the last two sentences typifies an *instrumentalist* view of science. The approach taken by

Locke, on the other hand, is termed *scientific realism*. The difference between these two views is crucial for our estimate of the metaphysical significance of science. If scientific realism is accepted, then good scientific theories are our closest approximation to the literal truth about "what there is"; but on an instrumentalist view science may have very little metaphysical significance. So let us proceed to clarify the different views.

Scientific realism may be defined as the view that *scientific theories are intended to be literally true, and accepting a theory involves believing that it gives a true description of reality*. Some further clarifications are needed, however. Note first of all that theories are "intended to be" literally true. A scientific realist would not commit himself to saying that our current theories actually *are* literally true, for he is well aware that science changes and that the current theories may and indeed probably will be replaced by better ones; science is an unending enterprise. One might say, therefore, that the scientific realist is committed more to the *scientific enterprise* as a way of finding the truth about the world than to any particular set of scientific *results*. However, scientific realists typically believe that the best existing theories represent at least a *close approximation* to the truth about the world. (Newtonian mechanics, for example, would still be recognized as such a close approximation in spite of the fact that, strictly speaking, it has been superseded by relativity theory and quantum mechanics.)

Scientific realism can also be defined as the view according to which *physical objects have those properties, and only those properties, which are attributed to them by the best attainable scientific theories*. Thus there is a clear-cut opposition between scientific realism and common-sense realism. The latter states that physical objects have the properties which *we perceive them to have,* while the former denies that objects have those properties and claims that they have other, "scientific" properties instead.

Instrumentalism, on the other hand, states that *scientific theories are not intended to be literally true, and accepting a theory requires us to believe only that its observational consequences are true.* Here the notion of "observational consequences" needs clarification. Science is based on observations; and unless the statements of those observations are taken as *true,* science has no basis. But, the instrumentalist reminds us, it is necessary to be quite clear about what exactly it is that we observe.

In some cases this presents no problem—as when an ethologist observes a group of animals behaving in a certain way. Often, however, observations are made with the aid of instruments— say, an ammeter or a Geiger counter. In these cases, the instrumentalist insists, what we literally observe is a *state of the measuring instrument,* a pointer reading on the ammeter or Geiger counter. The aim of science is to *predict* such pointer readings correctly, and thus enable us to manipulate nature for our technological ends. Science itself is an "instrument" for the prediction and control of nature. In carrying out this aim, scientists have found it convenient to talk about unobservable objects, such as atoms, molecules, electric currents and gamma rays. These unobservable objects, however, need not be taken as real entities, nor need statements about them be assumed to be literally true. They are, rather, best seen as mere calculational devices, conveniences which assist the scientist to express in the simplest, most economical way the relationships between pointer readings. As William James puts it,

> It is . . . *as if* reality were made of ether, atoms or electrons, but we musn't think so literally. The term "energy" doesn't even pretend to stand for anything "objective." It is only a way of measuring the surface of phenomena so as to string their changes on a simple formula.[3]

Which view is better? One advantage of instrumentalism is that it does not conflict with common-sense realism. We can go right on thinking that our everyday statements about the world are literally true and that roses really are red, violets really blue, and sugar really sweet. Science is fully accepted, in its proper sphere, but it does not give us any special, hitherto unknown information about the real nature of the world.

Another advantage of instrumentalism is that it is a more *cautious* view than realism. Instrumentalism allows the scientist to erect a theoretical structure which is as complex as necessary, but instrumentalism does not commit itself to the *truth* of those elements of the structure which go beyond what is actually observed. It is a more *empirical* way of viewing science. In support of this approach, instrumentalists point to the stormy history of science, in which the well-entrenched theories of one generation are the discredited outcasts of the next. One who commits himself, on the basis of such theories, to a view about the nature of ultimate reality will adopt a metaphysic as ephemeral as the scientific theories on which it is based.

On the other hand, it is worth pointing out that most (not all) working scientists seem to adopt a realist perspective on their work. They seem, that is, to take the attitude that in constructing their theories they are figuring out how things really work, not merely setting up calculational devices that will make it easier to compute the relationships between pointer readings. Of course, the fact that a scientist views her work in a certain way does not, by itself, prove that that is the correct way to view it. But the point still seems worth making.

There is also a problem for instrumentalism concerning the limits of what is "observable." The instrumentalist, as we have seen, must consider *observation statements* as being literally true; otherwise science would have no basis. It is the statements about *unobservable entities* which are seen as merely calculational tools rather than literal assertions about reality. Now in order for this to work, there must be a clear-cut distinction between what is and is not observable.

But it has been argued that no such distinction can be drawn. Consider the following series: observing something with the naked eye, observing it through a magnifying glass, through a low-power microscope, through a high-power microscope, through an electron microscope or in a Wilson cloud chamber. At each step in the sequence the observation becomes less direct, and the intervening instrumentation more complex. But at what point is one justified in drawing a line and saying that the items prior to this point in the series are "really observed" and thus exist in reality, whereas those after this point are "only theoretical" and have no real existence? Would it be sensible, for example, to say that chromosomes (visible in a high-powered microscope) are actual objects but that DNA chains (studied by electron microscopy) are not?

It should be pointed out that the scientific realist is not unaware of the history of science, but he draws a different moral from it than the instrumentalist. Someone who, on the basis of the phlogiston theory of combustion, accepted the real existence of phlogiston believed thereby a falsehood. But the trouble here is not with scientific realism but with the phlogiston theory. Of course, it is conceivable that some presently accepted theories are as wrong as the phlogiston theory, so one should be wary about accepting as literally true theories which are new and untested, or which have only flimsy experimental support. In this limited sense an instrumentalist attitude may be the correct one; a scientist may adopt a working hypothesis and stick with it for a long time without concluding anything as to its ultimate truth.

Yet it would seem that instrumentalists sometimes exaggerate the instability of scientific theory. Chemical theory has changed greatly since the time of Lavoisier, yet his reasons for abandoning phlogiston in favor of oxygen still strike us as sound, and a return in the future to something like the phlogiston theory is really inconceivable. Copernicus, Kepler, Newton and Einstein all presented different, and in certain respects incompatible, theories of celestial mechanics. Yet it is indisputable that they are all in fundamental agreement against pre-Copernican theories. Moreover their differences strike us as progressive rather than as a mere random succession of incompatible viewpoints. It is true that there are revolutions in science, but the more mature branches of science, looked at in a broad view, present an impressive picture of the cumulative and progressive growth of knowledge.

What can be said on behalf of scientific realism? The basic argument for scientific realism (and against instrumentalism) parallels the argument given in the last section for the realism of physical objects as opposed to idealism. In both cases the opposed theories seem to fare equally well when measured by the criteria of logical consistency and factual adequacy. But in each case the realist theory seems far superior to its competitor in *explanatory power*. Thus we saw that idealism denies realism's contention that our sensory perceptions are the result of the action of real, independently existing physical objects on our sense organs, but it does not provide a satisfactory alternative explanation.

But how does this apply to scientific realism? Suppose you have picked up a "blip" on your Geiger counter. The scientific explanation for this is that an unstable atomic nucleus has split apart, emitting (among other things) a beta particle. This particle has interacted with the detection coil of the Geiger counter, inducing a small surge of electric current. This current, after having been amplified, is channeled into a speaker, and when the surge reaches the speaker the blip is heard. The *observed* phenomenon, the blip, is explained as the result of an entire chain of processes involving *unobservable* entities, including atomic nuclei, beta particles and electrons. This much is clear. But note that according to instrumentalism these unobserved entities and processes *do not really exist*. And if this is so, then no explanation for the blip has been given. Explanation by means of a fictitious mechanism is no explanation at all. In general, instrumentalism tends to drain theories of their explanatory power even as it preserves their skin of empirical observations.[4]

Explanatory power favors scientific realism in yet another way:

*Instrumentalism fails to explain the success of science in making pre-
dictions which are empirically adequate.* The point here is simple. If
there is indeed a real though unobservable mechanism underlying
some observable phenomenon, and a scientist has correctly understood that mechanism, then it is not too surprising if on the
basis of that understanding she is able to make predictions which
are experimentally verified. If, on the other hand, the postulated
mechanism is fictitious, then there is no reason to expect this. If
the postulation of a nonexistent mechanism enables her to make
accurate predictions of observable phenomena, this would seem
to be just lucky. But the progress of science needs some explanation other than luck.

This does not, to be sure, apply to all aspects of science with
equal force. When a scientific hypothesis has been derived simply
by correlating observational results, a theory of the underlying
mechanism may not be very relevant to the empirical success of
the hypothesis. Thus the Boyle-Charles Law was derived without
reference to the kinetic theory of gases, although the kinetic theory contributes greatly to our understanding of why the Boyle-
Charles Law holds. But there are other cases in which a theory
enables a scientist to predict a *qualitatively new* phenomenon, one
which there is no reason to expect apart from the theory itself.
When such a prediction is made, the theory is on the line: If the
prediction fails, the theory will be discredited; but if it succeeds,
there will be a strong tendency to recognize it, not merely as empirically correct, but as *true* about the way the world works. For
how else could one explain that prediction?[5]

Let me conclude this section with an example. According to the
Big Bang theory of cosmology, the universe as we now know it
originated around fifteen billion years ago. At first all of the matter in the universe was concentrated in an extremely dense state;
a sort of cosmic explosion (the "Big Bang") sent it hurtling out in
all directions, leading eventually to the formation of the stars, star
clusters, nebulae and galaxies as we know them. Now, one predic-

tion of the Big Bang theory was that some of the radiation produced in that original explosion should *still exist today*. When the
prediction was first made (in the 1940s) no such radiation was
known to exist, nor was any detected for a long time thereafter. In
fact, the prediction came to be viewed as an embarrassment to the
theory. But finally, in 1965, a pair of scientists using a radio telescope for an entirely different purpose discovered the "cosmic
background radiation." This radiation is now regarded as one of
the principal confirmations of the Big Bang theory—as well it
might be. And is there not something awesome in the thought
that we today, using a properly attuned radio telescope, can still
"hear" the echoes of that majestic event by which the universe
was formed?

Consequences of Scientific Realism

Suppose that, moved by these considerations, we adopt the perspective of scientific realism and accept our best current scientific
theories as (provisional) indications of the real nature of the
world. What metaphysical consequences flow from this acceptance? There are two sorts of consequences, negative and positive. We shall briefly consider each in turn.

The negative consequence is that we shall have to admit that in
themselves roses are *not* red, violets are *not* blue, sugar is *not*
sweet. We shall have to admit, that is, that many of the perceptual
properties of objects are not really properties of the objects themselves. It might be thought that this could be avoided. The loss
of explanatory power in scientific theories, emphasized in the last
section, occurs only if we deny the real existence of the theoretical
entities to which they refer. But why can't we *admit* the reality
of those entities and at the same time affirm that physical objects
also have the properties attributed to them by sense perception
and common-sense realism?

This, however, is not really a viable option. For one thing, we
would still be left with the problem developed in the first section

of this chapter: Physical objects are experienced differently by different kinds of perceivers, and there is no nonarbitrary way to single out one set of perceptual properties as the properties really possessed by the object. But the more fundamental point is that the perceptual properties thus introduced would be, scientifically speaking, entirely redundant: They have no role to play in the explanation of the perceptual process. For example, the fact that I see the color of a rose is explained scientifically in terms of photons of certain energy levels that are reflected by the rose, focused by the lens of my eye and registered on the rods and cones of my retina. The resulting information is transmitted along my optic nerve and processed in my brain, resulting in the experience of color. To say that *in addition* to reflecting those photons the rose *also* is orange-red in color violates the requirement of simplicity by adding a property which has no explanatory value. I don't see the rose as orange-red because it "really is" that color; I see it thus because it reflects those particular kinds of photons.

So scientific realism is right about the properties of physical objects. Is this a disappointing conclusion? Does it mean, as suggested in our discussion of Locke, that objects exist in the world stripped of all the properties that make them interesting and valuable? Not really.

Note first of all that it is not correct to say that violets are not blue, sugar is not sweet, roses are not fragrant. The perceptual properties of objects are not illusory! What *is* true is that sugar *in itself* is not sweet, but to this we must add that sugar *is* sweet *to the taste of normal human beings*. The property of sweetness, then, is *relational;* it characterizes the interaction between the molecular structure of sugar and the human sense organs and brain. And so for other perceptual properties. The world *as experienced by humans* has all of the familiar sensory properties which help to keep life interesting.

Still, the "scientific" properties of objects are metaphysically more fundamental than the sensory properties. If we were to encounter a race of intelligent extraterrestrials, it is possible that we would have great difficulty in communicating to them the content of our sensory experiences, and they to us. Perhaps they simply *will not experience* the redness of roses and the sweetness of sugar; and, on the other hand, they may experience other sorts of sensory qualities of which we have no conception. But the physical properties of electromagnetic radiation and the chemical structure of the sugar molecule will be the same for them as for us: They represent the real nature of the world. (In one science-fiction story the key to the language of a perished race of Martians—the Martian "Rosetta Stone," so to speak—is found when someone discovers on the wall of an abandoned classroom the Martian version of the periodic table of the elements!)

The chief positive benefit of scientific realism for metaphysics is that if this perspective is accepted, a great deal of our best scientific knowledge becomes metaphysical knowledge as well. Science will be, quite literally, "falsifiable metaphysics." Scientific theories will be not merely calculational devices for predicting experimental results and promoting better technology (though they are that), but valid insights into the nature of reality.

In order to appreciate the importance of this, one needs some knowledge (not necessarily expert knowledge) of the various branches of science and their results. One is then confronted with a breath-taking panorama ranging from the minuteness of the subatomic realm to the immensity of the known universe. The time scale of creation ranges from particles whose lives are measured in billionths of a second to objects whose existence spans millions, hundreds of millions, even billions of years. The principles of construction range from the exquisite simplicity of crystalline structures to the rich complexity of interrelationships in an ecological community. Each person, no doubt, will react to this panorama in his or her own way, but for the Christian the response must certainly be, "Lord, manifold are thy works; in wisdom hast thou made them all."

However we may respond to it, this scientific picture of the world has to rank as one of the major accomplishments of our civilization. And the thought may occur to us, Could this scientific world picture be the grand design, the overall scheme of things, for which Tennyson was yearning when he wrote the poem cited at the beginning of this chapter?

Probably not—not if one wishes, as Tennyson did, to "know what God and man is." About God there is no question: God is not a scientific object. He cannot be caught in the web of our scientific theories nor subjected to controlled experimentation. Concerning man, the question is disputed. A great many scientists and philosophers share a faith that when the scientific world picture is complete, human life in all its aspects will be completely explained and understood within it. Indeed, they believe that man's existence will be completely explained within the framework of physics, biology and biochemistry, very much along the lines of these sciences as they presently exist.

I have characterized this as a faith, for that is what it is. Our present science by no means provides such a comprehensive explanation for human existence, nor is it obvious that the future development of science must lead in this direction. (It is noteworthy that behaviorism, long the leading candidate for a scientific psychology, seems to be falling into decline; the movements that are replacing it are not so obviously reductionist and "scientistic." We need to remind ourselves that the dreams of scientists do not always come true.) Still, the faith remains. In chapters two and three we considered some of the perspectives on human nature which reflect this faith, principally scientific determinism, philosophical behaviorism and materialism. It was shown there that the arguments in support of these positions are far from conclusive and also that they are open to serious objections; the arguments will not be repeated here.

But even if the scientific world picture is not in itself a complete representation of the grand design of the universe, it can hardly help but be an important element in that design. Science may not provide a complete explanation of human existence, but it provides important insights into human life and behavior which cannot be ignored. And while God cannot be captured in the nets of our theories, those theories may, just possibly, help us apprehend and exhibit this world in which we live as the kind of world God could have created.

The Origin of the World

As a concrete illustration of the metaphysical implications of science, this chapter will conclude with some considerations concerning the origin and history of the universe. This has been recognized as an important metaphysical question since the beginnings of philosophy among the ancient Greeks. Does the universe exist, as Aristotle and many others have held, without any large-scale, overall change? If so, the cosmos could have a "history" only in its localized details; the overall structure would be (so far as we can tell) everlasting. Or is the universe a kind of cyclical process, undergoing major changes but at last, over vast periods of time, returning to the starting point? The ancient Stoics, among others, believed that the universe is periodically consumed by fire and then reborn. Or does the universe have a specific beginning point and a foreseeable ending? Only in this case would the universe have a history in the sense in which a human life has a history; it would have a beginning, a middle and an end. These questions, long a matter of metaphysical speculation, may now be receiving a scientific answer through the recently developed science of cosmology.

There are, in fact, definite considerations which suggest that the universe as we know it had its origin at a specific point in the past, probably between ten and twenty billion years ago. Two lines of reasoning will be mentioned.

First, the *second law of thermodynamics* states that in a closed physical system the entropy always tends to increase. What this means, roughly, is that the available energy in the system gets used up. The energy is not lost entirely, but it is diffused and is no longer available for doing any work. For example, when you drive your car the energy from the gasoline mostly becomes diffused through the atmosphere in the form of heat—the energy still exists, but there is no way that you can collect it and put it back into the tank for the next trip. In the same way, the radiant energy produced by a star becomes diffused throughout space and cannot be recaptured to make another star. The second law of thermodynamics states that this process is irreversible, that the stars, all of them, and eventually the universe as a whole will burn out, grow cold and die. And the fact that this has not already happened shows that the universe has been in existence only for a finite time.

The *expansion of the universe* also points to a definite beginning of things. It has been firmly established that the universe is expanding. Galaxies (such as our own Milky Way) are held together by gravitation and do not expand, and the same is true of some groups of galaxies. But beyond this, all of the more distant galaxies are continually receding from us (and we from them), and the rate of the expansion increases the more distant they are. In a sufficiently long time, then, all the distant galaxies will have disappeared from sight, leaving us in contact with only our own "local group." And if we extrapolate the expansion backward in time, we reach the Big Bang itself, the cosmic explosion in which the universe as we know it began.

There are alternatives to the Big Bang theory in modern cosmology, but they suffer from serious scientific weaknesses. The *steady-state cosmology* is a modern version of the idea that the universe as a whole is unchanging. The key idea is that as the universe expands and the distant galaxies pass out of sight, *new matter is continuously created in empty space*. This new matter (consisting of hydrogen atoms) then combines to form new stars and new galaxies to replace those which disappear. Stars and galaxies come and go, but the universe remains the same.

It should be stressed that the "continuous creation" of the steady-state theory has nothing to do with any religious concept of creation; the production of new matter out of nothing is supposed to be a function of *space itself*. This conception is entirely lacking in experimental support and seems to contradict established principles, including the conservation of mass-energy and the second law of thermodynamics. Thus it has been the target of a good deal of suspicion since the steady-state theory was first formulated.

But more recently observational evidence has mounted against this theory. Observations on the distribution of distant radio sources seem to confirm the predictions of the Big Bang theory and to disconfirm those of the steady-state theory. And the discovery of the cosmic background radiation, noted in the previous section, may well have been the decisive blow. From the standpoint of the steady-state theory, this discovery is entirely unexpected, whereas it confirms a crucial prediction of the Big Bang theory. As a result, steady-state cosmology has at present few defenders left.

Another alternative is the *theory of the oscillating universe*. This theory accepts the occurrence of the Big Bang but predicts that the expansion will eventually be halted and reversed by the mutual gravitational attraction of the matter in the universe. The resulting "big crunch" is followed by another big bang, and the entire process starts over again. Thus we have a contemporary version of the Stoic doctrine of cosmic cycles: Each cycle lasts for a finite (though very long) period, but the universe as a whole has neither beginning nor end.

Unlike the steady-state theory, the cyclical theory still enjoys considerable support from scientists. Yet it too faces serious problems. Whether the cyclic rebirth can occur depends on two questions: Will there be a "big crunch"? And if there is, will it be followed by another expansion? The answer to the first question depends on the overall density of matter in the universe. If a certain critical density is exceeded, gravitational attraction will eventually halt and reverse the expansion; but if the density is below this level, the expansion will continue indefinitely. The evidence is not all in on this question, but what evidence there is strongly suggests that the actual density is below the critical density and that the expansion will continue.

But if a contraction were to occur, would it be followed by another expansion? The truth is that *there is no known scientific mechanism by which this could occur.* Speculations about another expansion resemble those of the steady-state theory, in that both must postulate novel physical processes whose existence is supported neither by observation nor by accredited scientific theory. Our best existing theory and evidence support the contention that the history of our universe has a definite beginning and a foreseeable end.

What conclusions should be drawn from all this? It would, I believe, be rather rash to claim that the creation of the universe by God has now been proved. For one thing, it needs to be emphasized that what has been said is based on the present state of scientific knowledge, and while the conclusions seem reasonably firm, future changes cannot be ruled out.[6] But even more important, the *most* that could be proved, scientifically, by these cosmological reasonings is that as we trace back the history of our universe we reach a point at which scientifically we can go no further. That *God* was the Creator, the Instigator of this process, is a conclusion to which scientific reasoning cannot attain.

On the other hand, could not the fact that scientific reasoning reaches such a "beginning point" itself be taken as a confirmation of the metaphysical hypothesis that the Lord God created the heavens and the earth out of nothing? How better (humanly speaking) could God have done this? Is it possible, then, that the Big Bang is simply the way creation looks from here?[7]

5

God and
the World

G od is more—much more—
than a problem in metaphysics. Believing in God, that is, having
faith in God, is much more than merely believing that God exists.
Knowing God is much more than knowing certain metaphysical
truths about God, more indeed than knowing anything at all
about God. The knowledge and love of God has a personal and
existential dimension which goes far beyond ordinary knowledge
of whatever kind and penetrates to every corner of one's life and
being. But having faith in God does involve believing that God
exists, and it is not possible to know God in the personal and existential sense without knowing some truths about God. And God,
in addition to the innumerable other things that he is and does, is
also a topic for metaphysical reflection. God is true being, the
source of all being, the creator of all things which exist other than
himself—and these are concepts of great metaphysical significance. So it is not only appropriate but inevitable that a study of

metaphysics should involve a consideration of this topic.

God and Metaphysics

Metaphysical considerations about God generally take one of three forms. One of these consists of *arguments for the existence of God*. Metaphysics asks, What kinds of philosophical reasons are there for believing that God exists? A person who asks this need not, though she may, be trying to find out for herself whether there is a God or not. She may already be fully convinced, for personal and religious reasons, of the reality of God; still she asks whether there are *also* good reasons to believe in God which are based on ordinary rational considerations and are accessible to any reasonable human being regardless of prior religious commitment. This, I think, is an entirely sensible question. And pursuing it, whether or not it affects the strength of one's belief, can bring great philosophical rewards.

Most of the arguments which have been proposed fall into a few general types. *Ontological arguments* set out to prove that it is logically impossible that God should not exist—that the denial of God's existence is self-contradictory. *Cosmological arguments* reason to God's existence from the bare existence of the universe, apart from consideration of any special features it may contain. If anything exists at all, these arguments claim, then God must exist. *Design arguments* (also called *teleological arguments*) reason from the order, beauty and apparent design of the universe and its contents to God as the designing intelligence. *Moral arguments* reason in various ways from our experience as moral beings to the existence of God as the source and guarantor of the moral law. These are the general types, but there are numerous arguments of each type, and perhaps even a few that do not fall into any of these categories.

The arguments for God's existence will not be further considered in this book, even though they constitute an important metaphysical topic. But I am convinced that a discussion of these arguments must be fairly thorough in order to be worthwhile, and for that the space is simply not available. Discussions of the arguments can be found in any standard work on the philosophy of religion.[1]

A second group of metaphysical questions concerns the *attributes of God.* "God is a Spirit," says the Westminster Catechism, "infinite, eternal, and unchangeable in his being, wisdom, power, justice, holiness, goodness, and truth." These attributes are not only of great religious importance, but they also raise questions for metaphysics. Philosophical consideration of the divine attributes can take one of two forms. Sometimes philosophers, having to their satisfaction established by argument that God exists, go on to prove that God has certain properties or characteristics.

In recent philosophy, however, the attributes are more often treated hypothetically, as was done in chapter two. That is to say, the philosopher does not try to prove that God has certain attributes, but rather he accepts the attributes as assertions about God made by theology and proceeds to ask philosophical questions about them. Examples of such questions are these: How should the attribute of omnipotence be defined? Is the attribute a logically possible one—that is, free from internal contradiction? Is it consistent with other divine attributes? What does it imply concerning God's relationship with his creation? Such questions are of great importance for both metaphysics and theology. But, like the arguments for God's existence, they cannot be discussed further here because of space limitations.[2]

A third group of metaphysical questions about God concerns the *relationship between God and the world.* The major views of God's nature suggest different ways of conceiving this relationship. *Theism* conceives of God as the personal creator of the world, the source and sustainer of all things other than himself who is completely self-sufficient and independent of the things he has created. *Pantheism,* on the other hand, conceives of God and the world as identical—God and the universe are the very same thing considered from different points of view. *Panentheism,* in many ways a compromise or intermediate view between theism and pantheism, holds that all things that exist are "in God" and indeed parts of God, and yet God has a unity and identity of his own distinct from that of his finite parts. It is with these viewpoints, the similarities and contrasts between them, and their respective strengths and weaknesses, that this chapter will be chiefly concerned. For the sake of completeness, however, we begin with a view which asserts that there is no relationship between God and the world: There is no God, and the world is complete and self-sufficient on its own.

Naturalism: The World without God

Philosophical *naturalism* insists that the natural world is complete in itself, self-contained and self-sufficient. According to naturalism, everything which exists or occurs lies entirely within the domain of natural processes. Nothing comes into nature or influences it from outside. There is no "outside"; nature is all there is.

Naturalists in general are tremendously impressed with the progress and success of science, not least with its success in vanquishing superstition, including magic, astrology and religion. Naturalism's strength, then, lies in its appropriation of scientific knowledge and scientific explanation as these apply to the natural world. God, since he does not exist, presents no problem for naturalism. Man, on the other hand, is naturalism's greatest challenge. As we have noted several times already, up until now strictly scientific approaches to human life and behavior have been much less successful than those same approaches have been when applied to subhuman nature. This is not to deny that many valuable insights have been gained. But the "grand synthesis" which will unify the sciences of man in a way comparable to the "Newtonian synthesis" in physics is not yet in sight. The naturalist will respond that this is due primarily to the greater complexity of human phenomena; a contributing factor, he may add, is the resistance created by the prevalence of nonscientific (that is, nonnaturalistic) ways of viewing human beings.

Naturalism typically expresses itself in metaphysics through such viewpoints as behaviorism, mind-body identity theory and scientific determinism. The debates over these viewpoints are, at bottom, debates over the adequacy of a naturalistic understanding of human life. The naturalist is likely to feel that, whatever the difficulties and obscurities of particular points, the naturalistic understanding of man is obviously correct and the resistance to it is the result of sentimentality and superstition. To the nonnaturalist, on the other hand, it may appear equally obvious that the naturalist is interpreting human life within a restricted and rather rigid conceptual scheme in spite of abundant evidence that the concepts are not adequate for the subject matter. The deep feelings on both sides of this issue are one reason why philosophical agreement is so difficult to achieve.

Pantheism: God as Identical with the World

According to *pantheism* in its simplest form, God and the universe are identical. Other formulations say that God is identical not with the totality of all beings but with the "ground of being," the "power of being," or the basic structure of reality. It is sometimes debated whether these doctrines should also be called pantheism or not, but for our purposes this is not a question of much importance. What is important is that in all of these versions the divine is identified not with some particular, concrete being or beings, but as a sort of universal presence somehow diffused throughout all things but nowhere existing as an individual entity.

It is important to understand some of the religious motivations for pantheism. Probably pantheism most often makes its appeal to persons who, having "grown beyond" popular, literalistic forms of religion, nevertheless do not wish to see the divine banished from their world entirely. So their religion becomes a kind of general reverence for "the God in everything." This is easier for some sophisticated persons to accept than the more concrete beliefs of theistic religions. Typically the divine is seen as providing some sort of validation and support for values such as truth, beauty and goodness. The most typical religious attitude for the pantheist is one of resting in, and identifying with, the "universal presence." Pantheism also readily lends itself to the forms of mysticism in which the individual is said to be submerged or swallowed up in the divine.

From the standpoint of theism, the religious deficiencies of pantheism are marked. The pantheistic God is the "power of being" in everything, but it cannot do any particular thing. It is thought of as the source of value, and yet its universality and lack of concrete individuality suggest that it cannot really discriminate between good and evil. Indeed, a common pantheistic tenet is that in God good and evil (or "what *we call* good and evil") are ultimately reconciled in a "higher harmony." And this is very nearly to say that God is indifferent to the distinction between good and evil. We may, if we will, pray to the pantheistic God, but not with the expectation that it hears our prayers or will do anything to answer them. It can be the object of human thoughts, attitudes and actions; but it never itself acts in any way.

From a philosophical standpoint, the first question to ask about pantheism is what it *means*. To put it bluntly, how is reality any different if pantheism is true than if there is no God at all? At least two claims are involved: (1) the universe is a unity, and (2) this unity is divine. Are these claims defensible?

Considering what is known of the universe, it is hard to see how it is a unity in any stronger sense than that it is a single space-time continuum in which things are interrelated according to a single set of natural laws. This kind of unity, however, does not seem to offer much support for the religious attitudes which pantheists wish to direct to their God. Spinoza, with his "intellectual love of God," went about as far as anyone could in worshiping the system of nature as it is revealed to us by mechanistic science. But while many feel admiration for Spinoza and his philosophy, few have found it in their hearts to worship his God. All in all, it would seem that pantheists need to be a good deal clearer than they have generally succeeded in being about *what* it means to say that the universe is divine and *why* we should worship it, hold it in reverence or adopt religious attitudes toward it.

Panentheism: God as Including the World

Panentheism agrees with pantheism that everything which exists is part of God, yet it does not simply identify God with the totality of things. All things are part of God, yet he has a unity and identity of his own which is not simply that of his finite parts. God is not identical with the cosmos, but neither is he separated from it. Rather, he lives his own life in and through it: The world is God's body. And we ourselves are parts of God. All our experiences are also his experiences, so that he is, in Whitehead's words, "the great companion—the fellow-sufferer who understands."[3]

Perhaps the best way to grasp this is through an analogy. Suppose, for a moment, that each cell in your body possesses a consciousness, a center of awareness, of its own. Each cell, then, would be aware of the organic processes in its immediate environment and would have, through this, a very limited and obscure apprehension of what is happening to the body as a whole. In addition to all these individual, cellular awarenesses, there is also *your mind,* the awareness which "draws together" all of the "cellular minds" and expresses them in a unified awareness of your entire body. Your mind *includes* the various cellular minds, but it also *transcends* them in a "unity of the whole." It is in some such way as this that panentheism conceives of the relationship between our minds and the mind of God.

The motivations for accepting panentheism are various, but a common theme runs through most of them. Panentheism seeks to retain many of the religious resources of theism while at the same time avoiding the dichotomy or separation between God and the world which characterizes traditional theism. The doctrine that all things are "in God" overcomes this dichotomy while it avoids simply identifying God with the cosmos. Panentheism acknowledges that certain aspects of God's being are unchangeable, but it stresses God's involvement in temporal processes in a way that is meant to correct what is felt to be classical theism's overemphasis on the immutability of God. And the doctrine that God shares all our experiences is intended to bring God closer to humanity and to correct the classical doctrine that God is "impassible," unsusceptible to emotion. God is God, but God is also deeply involved in all that happens in the lives of his world and his children.

In its current form panentheism is a relative newcomer to the philosophical and theological scene. Drawing its inspiration from the philosophies of A. N. Whitehead and Charles Hartshorne, it has attained considerable prominence and influence through the theological movement known as *process theology*.[4] Because it is such a comparatively recent development, the evaluation of "process theism" is by no means complete. Still it is possible to make some tentative observations.

It would seem, to begin with, that God as conceived by panentheism is in principle capable of doing and being many of the things that are attributed to God by Christianity. God is sufficiently distinct from the world to be capable of thinking about it and acting upon it, and sufficiently distinct from us that it is possible for us to enter into a relationship with him. There may be difficulties on these points related to specific formulations of process philosophy and theology, but it seems that process theism may be able to give an account of God as a thinking, acting and relational being. And the complaint that classical theism has overemphasized the immutability and the remoteness of God finds a corrective in panentheism.

On the other hand, the doctrine that we are all "part of God" may create difficulties for Christian theology. Does this mean that, in saving us from our sins, God is literally *saving himself*? This would seem to be implied, yet this notion strikes Christians as strange. And if not all are saved, does this mean that part of God is irretrievably damned? If so, one can understand why process theologians tend to be universalists! Process theologians certainly do not wish to affirm that God is the agent in human actions; they are quite clear in affirming free will in the libertarian sense. How then can it be said that our experiences are literally God's experiences?

The doctrine that the world is God's body also creates difficulties. Like the pantheist, the panentheist has to face the question of the degree to which the world as a whole can be considered to be a unity. Certainly our science does not discern in the cosmos as a whole anything remotely approaching the degree of unity and organization which exists in even the simplest organic body. In view of this, it might seem that the notion of the world as God's body is little more than a rather badly strained metaphor. Yet it has disturbing implications. To say that the world is God's body implies that God *needs the world* to live his life just as we need our bodies. And this means that God can never have existed without a world: Our present universe may, possibly, have a beginning and an end, but if so there must be an *infinite series of universes* throughout infinite past and future time. And this would seem to undermine fatally the doctrine of God's *self-sufficiency*, his *independence* from the world he has created, which is so important for traditional theism.

As has been already stated, process theism is a relatively new development, and the task of evaluating its implications remains a challenging one. As things now stand, it presents itself as a serious alternative to classical theism, as well as a challenge to rethink and restate theism's meaning and implications.

Theism: God as Creator of the World

Without doubt *theism,* the belief in a personal God who is the
Creator of the world, will for many readers be the most familiar
of the viewpoints considered in this chapter. Yet its implications
are not always clearly seen, and some of them may become more
apparent as theism is contrasted with other views. Theism, of
course, disagrees sharply with naturalism, maintaining that the
universe in general and human beings in particular are not independent and self-sufficient, but rather totally dependent on the
God in whom "we live, and move, and have our being." And theism's affirmation of the reality of God also allows it to take seriously the dimensions of human life which naturalism either mini-
mizes or denies entirely.

Theism's opposition to pantheism is hardly less intense than its
rejection of naturalism. Indeed, pantheism often seems to the
theist to be nothing more than a disguised naturalism overlaid
with a veneer of religious language. A God which is indistin-
guishable from the universe cannot really care for us, have a plan
for our lives, hear and answer our prayers, or save us from our
own wrongdoing. In certain respects the theist may even find
naturalism preferable to pantheism. A naturalist, at least, rejects
religion and religious values in a forthright and direct manner. A
pantheist, in contrast, makes what seem to be substantive religious assertions, but when closely examined the substance tends
to disappear, leaving behind only a vague aura of pious emotion.
In pantheism's favor it may be said that the pantheist typically
shows serious concern for those aspects of human existence which
are minimized by naturalism. But whether pantheism provides
an adequate framework for understanding human life in its full-
ness is open to serious question.

Theism's relationship to panentheism is more complex than its
rejection of naturalism and pantheism. Panentheism, in fact, has
come forward as a revised and improved version of theism ("neo-
classical theism," according to Hartshorne), and so it is to be ex-

pected that they would agree at many points. Specifically, both affirm a supreme God who is the source and sustainer of the universe and all it contains and whose purposes include the enrichment and fulfillment of human life.

The differences, however, are considerable. Perhaps the most fundamental is theism's stress on the *independence* and *self-sufficiency* of God, which panentheism seriously modifies and compromises. Classical theism stresses a *one-sided dependence* of the creation on the Creator, while panentheism tends to see them as *interdependent.* Theism may, indeed, wish to incorporate some of the emphasis on God as "sympathizing," as "feeling with us" in our pains and sorrows—thus modifying the traditional doctrine of God's impassivity. But Whitehead's characterization of God as the "fellow-sufferer who understands" carries a little too strongly the suggestion that, just as God sympathizes with us, we also ought to sympathize with him. However that may be, God's feelings toward us are those of the Creator toward his creation; according to theism we are not in any true sense "parts" of God.

Theism also will reject the notion of the universe as the "body" of God. God, to be sure, controls each part of the universe as readily as—and far more completely than—we control our own bodies. But in other respects the metaphor has little to recommend it. In particular, the idea that God "needs" the world in order to fulfill his own life is sharply rejected by theism. God needs nothing outside himself, and so it is wrong to say (as is sometimes said even in orthodox Christian circles) that God "was lonely" and "needed our companionship" and therefore created us. God is, after all, according to Christianity, the Trinity of Father, Son and Holy Spirit. Is it to be supposed that their eternal companionship lacks something which could be made up by human beings?

Many of these points can be summed up by saying that theism alone, among the viewpoints considered, affirms in its full sense the *creation* of the world by God. This creation is a creation *ex nihilo,* "out of nothing," and is an action sheerly of grace and generosity on God's part. If instead we see the creation as *ex deo,* "out of God's own nature," and as fulfilling a need on God's part, then the doctrine of God's grace in creation has been nullified. And since the doctrine of creation is an indispensable presupposition for the doctrine of redemption, it seems all too likely that such a change in the conception of creation will have repercussions on the doctrine of saving grace.

It is also of interest to note that of our four viewpoints only theism is prepared to welcome the notion of an absolute beginning of the universe as implied by Big Bang cosmology. Such an absolute beginning is incompatible with both naturalism and pantheism, and while panentheism may allow that the *present* universe has a beginning and an end, there is nothing in panentheism itself which would particularly lead one to expect this. Theists, on the other hand, have rather consistently maintained that the universe has a temporal beginning. It is, to be sure, just possible (and theistic philosophers have so argued) that theism is *consistent* with the notion of an eternal creation. But the biblical statements on creation, if taken at face value, clearly imply a temporal beginning, and this has also been affirmed by the creeds and theologians of the church—even those who, like Thomas Aquinas, could find no philosophical reason for denying the eternity of the world. So the absolute beginning of Big Bang cosmology is a datum which is not only admirably explained by theism but also, in a sense, fulfills a prediction made by theism.[5]

It would be a serious mistake to assume that the meaning of theism has been fixed definitively, "once and for all"—say, by the New Testament or by some classical theologian such as Thomas Aquinas—so that now it can be repeated, restated and defended but not modified in any way. The New Testament is fundamental and, for Christians, definitely authoritative. But it leaves many important issues as challenges for our further thinking. The theism of Aquinas is in many respects different from that of the New

Testament; it is for us to inquire whether it is a faithful and appropriate development of biblical doctrine, or a distortion of it, or perhaps both at once in different ways. Process theism may seem in certain respects to be inconsistent with biblical perspectives; it must all the same be studied, as Thomas studied the theism of the pagan Aristotle, for the insights it may afford. Without doubt the future will bring fresh challenges and fresh discoveries. God is God and his truth is eternal, but our apprehension of that truth is fallible, changing and, it is to be hoped, by his grace capable of growth.

Epilog
A Christian Metaphysic?

*I*s there a Christian metaphysic? According to Whitehead, "Christianity has always been a religion seeking a metaphysic."[1] What he meant by this is that Christianity came into the world as a religion of salvation rather than a metaphysical system; since then Christian thinkers have adopted a number of different systems but have failed to establish any one of them as definitive.

If Whitehead is right about this, then in at least two senses there is not and cannot be such a thing as a Christian metaphysic. In the first place, there is no one metaphysical system which is definitively Christian, but rather a number of systems, all of them more or less inconsistent with each other and all of them more or less adequate to the content of Christian faith. But the fact that Christianity is a religion of *salvation* also suggests that in a sense no philosophical system can be fully Christian, because no philosophical system can express the unique content of Christianity.

Philosophy is, as we saw in chapter one, a discipline based on human reflection and human intellectual resources. But the message of salvation is not a discovery of human reflection. It comes to us by revelation, and Christians have consistently acknowledged that its central truths—the Incarnation of God in Jesus Christ, his atoning death for our sins, his resurrection from the dead, salvation by grace through faith—cannot be known by unassisted human thought. No metaphysical system can incorporate these truths without becoming something other than philosophy, and in this sense no metaphysical system can be fully and distinctly Christian.

But if Christianity is not a metaphysical system, it nevertheless implies metaphysical claims. And since very early times Christian thinkers have struggled to formulate these claims in philosophical terminology and to demonstrate their rational acceptability using philosophical methods. If by a Christian metaphysic we mean the result of such reflection, in which a Christian thinker seeks to develop a metaphysical system which is compatible with Christian faith and which is an adequate vehicle for the expression of Christian convictions, then not only is there a Christian metaphysic, but there are quite a few of them.

The ideas presented in this book in no way deserve to be called a system of Christian metaphysics. It is hoped, however, that our survey of some issues has helped to bring into focus some of the themes with which a Christian metaphysic must deal. In this epilog I shall summarize these briefly, both as a way of tying together the contents of the book and in an attempt to clarify what Christian philosophy is about.

First, a Christian metaphysic must speak of *God*. God is the ultimate and supreme reality; he takes first place in our answer to the metaphysical question, "What is there?" And an adequate account of God's nature—at least, as adequate as possible—must be a high priority for Christian philosophy. Of the various conceptions of God considered in the last chapter, it seems clear that theism is the one which a Christian metaphysic should adopt and develop. Pantheistic tendencies have appeared from time to time within Christianity, but they have always been rejected as a serious aberration. And while panentheism merits some consideration as a Christian metaphysic, it would seem in view of the arguments presented earlier that its defects outweigh its advantages.

God, then, is the Sovereign and sole Creator, the supreme personal Being who has made the universe out of nothing for his own purposes and continues to be active in sustaining it and directing it toward its goal. More than this, God is the Savior and Redeemer, drawing all people to himself through the death of his Son. Concerning this great gift philosophy cannot speak—yet it should never be far from the thoughts of one who would endeavor to construct a Christian metaphysic.

A Christian metaphysic must also speak of *creation*. God is true Being, but he has not selfishly kept to himself the privilege of existence. Rather he freely bestows it on sun and moon and stars, on fields and forests, on beasts and birds and flowers. And it is important, in recognition of God's creative work, that we recognize these his creatures as *real* beings, not independent of the God who created them, but having a solid and substantial existence of their own. So it would seem that realism concerning the physical world is the appropriate stance for the Christian to take, in spite of the fact that idealism has often been presented as a Christian metaphysic. The position of scientific realism, advocated in chapter four, is not obligatory for a Christian metaphysician, but it is consistent with a Christian conception of creation. Scientific realism should certainly not be taken to mean that God has not really created the fragrance and color of a rose or the taste of a peach. On the contrary, God *has* created these things, first by bringing into being biological structures with certain scientific properties, and then by creating human beings with the sense organs which, interacting with those biological structures, convey to us the experiences which so delight us.

As has been suggested already, I believe that much remains to be done by Christian philosophers in developing an adequate philosophical understanding of the natural world. Much of this work properly belongs to the philosophy of natural science, but it is also an unfinished task for metaphysics.

Finally, a Christian metaphysic must speak of *man as the image of God*. The phrase "the image of God" is used in a number of places in Scripture to indicate the unique likeness and relationship to God which sets humanity apart from the rest of the creation. No exposition of these passages will be attempted here; in any case the phrase has acquired a breadth of meaning which transcends what could be derived from the exegesis of specific verses. The phrase is best taken, I suggest, to denote the central characteristics which single man out and make him different from the other animals. These will not be physical characteristics—the human form, after all, is not so very different from that of an ape —but rather qualities of mind and spirit which make the human species truly unique. (Note that if there are indeed intelligent extraterrestrials sharing these capacities, then they also would bear the image of God. The qualities in question are uniquely human *in our experience,* but perhaps not absolutely.)

The qualities which make up God's image would include rationality, the ability to distinguish good from evil and to make moral choices, the capacity for deeply meaningful personal relationships and, above all, the capacity to know God—to conceive of God, to experience the need of God's presence, to enter into a relationship with God. While some of these characteristics seem to be foreshadowed in a limited way in some of the lower animals, when taken together they constitute a unique ensemble which sets man apart.

Certainly a proper appreciation of these human qualities requires much more than metaphysics, just as knowing God involves more than knowing metaphysical truths about God. But metaphysics has its role to play; an inadequate metaphysical interpretation of human nature can render these unique human characteristics unintelligible. A naturalistic view of man denies the significance of man's religious needs and capacities; determinism negates the possibility of free moral choices; materialism negates the eternal life which God has in store for us. In chapters two and three an attempt was made to suggest metaphysical perspectives on human nature which enable us to give the image of God in man its full meaning and value. Specific solutions may be debated, but the questions are urgent and the task of answering them is a vital one.

This then is metaphysics: a set of questions which press us to the very limits of human understanding, answers to those questions which are passionately held and yet deeply controversial, and in support of those answers seemingly endless arguments and counterarguments, rebuttals and counterrebuttals. The task of seeking understanding is indeed endless. May we all continue in it, as we seek to love God with all our minds.

Notes

Chapter One: Introducing Metaphysics

[1]Willard V. O. Quine, "On What There Is," in *From a Logical Point of View* (New York: Harper, 1963), p. 1. Quine uses the word "ontology" rather than "metaphysics," but for purposes here the terms may be regarded as synonyms.

[2]Actually I am already taking sides by assuming that there *are* basic or foundational truths: one school of epistemology, known as the "coherence theory," claims that *all* of our beliefs must be justified through their relationships to other things that we believe. For more on these issues, see the volume in this series entitled *Epistemology* by David Wolfe (Downers Grove, Ill.: InterVarsity Press, 1982).

[3]For the term "metaphysical data" I am indebted to Richard Taylor, *Metaphysics*, 2d ed. (Englewood Cliffs, N.J.: Prentice-Hall, 1974), pp. 2-4.

Chapter Two: Freedom and Necessity

[1]Robert Frost, "The Road Not Taken" in *The Complete Works of Robert Frost* (New York: Henry Holt, 1949), p. 131.

[2]*The Rubáiyát of Omar Khayyám*, 2d ver. #79, trans. Fitzgerald (New York: Walter J. Black, 1942), p. 89.

[3]Strictly speaking, these terms are not quite synonymous: soft determinism is

the view that determinism *is* true and is compatible with free will, while compatibilism implies only that determinism *may* be true.

[4]B. F. Skinner, *Walden Two* (New York: Macmillan, 1962), p. 257, Skinner's italics. Strictly speaking, the quotation is not from Skinner himself but from Frazier, the protagonist of the novel and Skinner's alter ego.

[5]Quoted in C. J. Ducasse, "Determinism, Freedom, and Responsibility," in S. Hook, ed., *Determinism and Freedom in the Age of Modern Science* (New York: Collier, 1961), pp. 160-61.

[6]Bertrand Russell and F. C. Copleston, "The Existence of God—A Debate," in P. Edwards and A. Pap, eds. *A Modern Introduction to Philosophy,* rev. ed. (New York: Free Press, 1965), p. 480.

[7]See "Bell's Theorem: Still Not Ringing True," *Science News* 120 (1981):117.

[8]René Descartes, "Principles of Philosophy," in *The Philosophical Works of Descartes,* vol. 1, trans. E. S. Haldane and G. R. T. Ross (Cambridge: Cambridge Univ. Press, 1931), prin. 41, p. 235.

[9]For recent discussions of this argument, see James N. Jordan, "Determinism's Dilemma," *Review of Metaphysics* 23 (1969-70):48-66; and William Hasker, "The Transcendental Refutation of Determinism," *Southern Journal of Philosophy* 11 (1973):175-83.

[10]The term "believe" is used in order to avoid certain technical problems, but if the reader finds the use of "believe" in connection with God too jarring, the word "know" may be substituted.

[11]Two important recent statements of the argument will be found in Arthur N. Prior, "The Formalities of Omniscience," in *Papers on Time and Tense* (Oxford: Oxford Univ. Press, 1968); and Nelson Pike, *God and Timelessness* (New York: Schocken, 1970), pp. 53-72. For an attempted answer, see Alvin Plantinga, *God, Freedom and Evil* (New York: Harper, 1974), pp. 65-73.

[12]There is another view which arrives at essentially the same result by a different route. This view states that future-tense statements (such as, "I will eat a cheese omelet tomorrow") are indeed already true or false. But it defines God's omniscience by saying that God knows all and only those truths which it is logically possible for him to know. And since (as is shown by the argument in the text) it is not logically possible for God to foreknow free human actions, God's failure to know the truth about my omelet in no way conflicts with his omniscience.

[13]Recent sympathetic expositions of the doctrine of timelessness include Richard L. Purtill, "Foreknowledge and Fatalism," *Religious Studies* 10 (1974); Eleonore Stump and Norman Kretzmann, "Eternity," *Journal of Philosophy* 78 (1981):429-58; and William Hasker, "Concerning the Intelligibility of 'God is Timeless,' " *The New Scholasticism* (Spring 1983).

Chapter Three: Minds and Bodies

[1]It should be noted that what is said here applies to *philosophical* behaviorism, not to behaviorism as a school of psychology. The psychological behaviorist advocates a behavioral *method* in psychology, which means among other things that psychologists should try to establish laws which deal with overt, observable behavior rather than with unobserved (but perhaps introspectable) "inner processes" in the mind. A philosophical behaviorist would in general tend to favor this behavioristic method in psychology, but a psychological behaviorist need not (though he may) have any views about philosophical behaviorism.

[2]Norman Malcolm, seeking to maintain a behavioristic analysis of dreaming, actually claims that (1) the question as to when, exactly, a dream occurred, has no clear sense, and that (2) it is meaningless even to talk about dreams which have occurred but have been totally forgotten (*Dreaming* [London: Routledge and Kegan Paul, 1959], pp. 70-82).

[3]See Karl Popper and John Eccles, *The Self and Its Brain* (New York: Springer, 1977), especially pp. 100-147 for more on this.

[4]For a readable account of current knowledge about the functional dependence of mind on brain, see Charles Furst, *Origins of the Mind: Mind-Brain Connections* (Englewood Cliffs, N.J.: Prentice-Hall, 1979).

[5]For more on this, see William Hasker, "The Souls of Beasts and Men," *Religious Studies* 10 (1974):265-67.

[6]Roger Penrose, "Black Holes," in *Cosmology Now,* ed. Laurie John (New York: Taplinger, 1976), p. 124.

[7]Wilder Penfield, *The Mystery of the Mind* (Princeton: Princeton Univ. Press, 1975), p. 215.

[8]For more on emergentism, see Hasker, "The Souls of Beasts and Men"; also William Hasker, "Emergentism," in *Religious Studies,* 1983. A version of dualism which seems compatible with emergentism is developed by Karl Popper in *The Self and Its Brain.* Somewhat similar views have also been developed by the neuroscientists Wilder Penfield and Roger Sperry.

[9]Examples of this view may be found in John Hick, *Philosophy of Religion,* 2d ed. (Englewood Cliffs, N.J.: Prentice-Hall, 1973), pp. 97-106; and Bruce Reichenbach, *Is Man the Phoenix?* (Washington, D.C.: Christian Univ. Press, 1978). These writers do not use the expression "Christian materialism," but it seems an apt designation for their view of human nature.

[10]*Philosophy of Religion,* pp. 100-101.

Chapter Four: The World

[1]Alfred Lord Tennyson, "Flower in the Crannied Wall."

[2]For details the reader is referred to George Pitcher, *Berkeley* (London: Routledge and Kegan Paul, 1977).

[3]"Pragmatism's Conception of Truth," in *Essays in Pragmatism* (New York: Hafner, 1969), p. 167, James's italics.

[4]In response to this it might be said that an instrumentalist could formulate scientific generalizations (for example, about the operation of Geiger counters) in purely observational terms, and then use these generalizations to explain the occurrence of a particular blip. Such an approach would avoid explanation by nonexisting mechanisms, but it is doubtful that this sort of explanation would be equal in explanatory power to the existing sciences with their reliance on theoretical entities. The fact is that it simply *has not proved feasible* to do science without theoretical entities: The instrumentalist is offering us a proposal about how science *might* be practiced rather than an account of science as it actually exists.

[5]For more on the realism-instrumentalism controversy, see Richard E. Grandy, ed., *Theories and Observations in Science* (Englewood Cliffs, N.J.: Prentice-Hall, 1973); Peter Smith, *Realism and the Progress of Science* (Cambridge: Cambridge Univ. Press, 1981); Bas C. van Fraassen, *The Scientific Image* (Oxford: Oxford Univ. Press, 1980); and Rom Harre, *Principles of Scientific Thinking* (Chicago: Univ. of Chicago Press, 1970).

[6]The need for caution at this point is underscored by the appearance of the new "inflationary" model of the early universe; this model preserves many central elements of the Big Bang theory but also diverges from it in important ways. (See Dietrick E. Thomsen, "The New Inflationary Nothing Universe," *Science News* 123 [12 Feb. 1983]:108-9.) This cosmological model is at present extremely speculative, and it is too early to assess either its scientific acceptability or its metaphysical implications.

[7]See Ernan McMullin, "Is Philosophy Relevant to Cosmology?" *American Philosophical Quarterly* 18 (1981):177-89; E. L. Schatzman, *The Structure of the Universe* (New York: McGraw-Hill, 1968); Laurie John, ed., *Cosmology Now* (New York: Taplinger, 1976); and Joseph Silk, *The Big Bang* (San Francisco: Freeman, 1980).

Chapter Five: God and the World

[1]See John Hick, *Philosophy of Religion*, 2d ed. (Englewood Cliffs, N.J.: Prentice-Hall, 1973); and William Rowe, *Philosophy of Religion: An Introduction* (Belmont, Calif.: Wadsworth, 1978); see also C. Stephen Evans, *Philosophy of Religion* (a volume in the Contours of Christian Philosophy series projected for release in late 1984).

[2]In addition to the books mentioned in the previous note, see Richard Swinburne, *The Coherence of Theism* (Oxford: Oxford Univ. Press, 1977); and Anthony Kenny, *The God of the Philosophers* (Oxford: Oxford Univ. Press, 1979).

[3]Albert North Whitehead, *Process and Reality*, Corrected Edition, ed. David

Ray Griffin and Donald W. Sherburne (New York: Free Press, 1978), p. 351.
⁴Sources on process theology include Whitehead, *Process and Reality;* Charles Hartshorne, *The Divine Relativity* (New Haven, Conn.: Yale Univ. Press, 1948); and John B. Cobb, Jr., and David Ray Griffin, *Process Theology: An Introductory Exposition* (Philadelphia: Westminster Press, 1976).
⁵But *only* "in a sense," since the failure to find scientific evidence for an absolute beginning would not count as a *disconfirmation* of theism. God could, after all, have created a "steady-state" universe or, for that matter, an "oscillating universe" at the beginning of its cycle. But both those models are readily *consistent* with an eternal cosmos, whereas the Big Bang theory is not.

Epilog: A Christian Metaphysic?
¹"Religion in the Making," in F. C. S. Northrup and Mason W. Gross, eds., *Alfred North Whitehead: An Anthology* (New York: Macmillan, 1953), p. 485.

Further Reading

The books listed here have been selected both for their philosophical value and their readability. The footnotes and bibliographies in these books will be valuable for students who wish to pursue some metaphysical problem in greater depth.

General books on metaphysics
Taylor, Richard. *Metaphysics*, 2d ed. Englewood Cliffs, N.J.: Prentice-Hall, 1974. Contains interesting, and sometimes provocative, discussions of a number of metaphysical questions. The reader is cautioned against trying to combine the conclusions of the various chapters into a consistent metaphysical system.

Walsh, W. H. *Metaphysics*. New York: Harcourt, Brace & World, 1963. A good general survey of the subject, with discussions of major metaphysical systems as well as of the opposition to metaphysics in some recent philosophy.

Free will and determinism
Campbell, C. A. *In Defense of Free Will*. New York: Humanities Press, 1967. The case for free will as presented by an important contemporary libertarian.

Dworkin, Gerald, ed. *Determinism, Free Will, and Moral Responsibility*. Englewood Cliffs, N.J.: Prentice-Hall, 1970. A well-chosen selection of essays representing all of the major points of view in the controversy.

The mind-body problem

Campbell, Keith. *Body and Mind*. Notre Dame, Ind.: Univ. of Notre Dame Press, 1980. A well-written and balanced discussion of several different theories, including behaviorism and dualism. The author favors central-state materialism as a tentative working hypothesis.

Lewis, Hywel D. *The Self and Immortality*. New York: Seabury Press, 1973. An interesting and readable discussion by a leading defender of dualism.

Popper, Karl, and Eccles, John. *The Self and Its Brain*. New York: Springer, 1977. A highly interesting collaboration between an eminent philosopher and an outstanding neuroscientist, who advocate dualism. The most accessible part of the book is the concluding section, a series of recorded dialogs between the authors.

Idealism and realism

Ewing, A.C. *The Fundamental Questions of Philosophy*. New York: Collier, 1962. The chapter entitled "Matter" is an excellent summary of the positions and arguments on this issue.

Pitcher, George, *Berkeley*. London: Routledge and Kegan Paul, 1977. A careful and detailed examination of Berkeley's view and his arguments for it.

Scientific realism and instrumentalism

Gale, George. *Theory of Science*. New York: McGraw-Hill, 1979. This book combines philosophical and historical approaches to science and contains good discussions of scientific realism and instrumentalism.

Harre, Rom. *Principles of Scientific Thinking*. Chicago: Univ. of Chicago Press, 1970. An effective statement of the realist view of scientific theories.

Nagel, Ernest. *The Structure of Science*. New York: Harcourt, Brace & World, 1961. The chapter entitled "The Cognitive Status of Theories" is a classical statement of an "irenic instrumentalist" viewpoint.

Philosophy of religion

Cobb, John B., Jr., and Griffin, David Ray. *Process Theology: An Introductory Exposition*. Philadelphia: Westminster, 1976. A good introduction to this important movement in theology and philosophy.

Peterson, Michael. *Evil and the Christian God*. Grand Rapids, Mich.: Baker, 1982. A lucid, readable and philosophically well-informed discussion of this important problem in the philosophy of theism.

Purtill, Richard L. *Reason to Believe*. Grand Rapids, Mich.: Eerdmans, 1974. An excellent introduction to the philosophy of religion for the general reader. Lucid and interestingly written, yet maintains high philosophical quality throughout.

Rowe, William L. *Philosophy of Religion,* Belmont, Calif.: Wadsworth, 1978. A carefully reasoned yet readable introduction to the major problems in the philosophy of religion.